WATER SAFETY

WATER SAFETY

From the Backyard Pool to the Open Ocean
How to Avoid and Survive Water Emergencies

BEN RAYNER

WATER SAFETY
FROM THE BACKYARD POOL TO THE OPEN OCEAN
HOW TO AVOID AND SURVIVE WATER EMERGENCIES

iUniverse books may be ordered through booksellers or by contacting:

iUniverse
1663 Liberty Drive
Bloomington, IN 47403
www.iuniverse.com
1-800-Authors (1-800-288-4677)

ISBN: 978-1-5320-2782-6 (sc)
ISBN: 978-1-5320-2783-3 (e)

Library of Congress Control Number: 2017912508

Print information available on the last page.

iUniverse rev. date: 08/16/2017

About the Author

Ben Rayner is a former underwater-egress and sea-survival instructor with Survival Systems USA, Inc., in Groton, Connecticut. A lifelong waterman, the author has been fortunate enough to have experienced many remote marine environments as a surfer, traveler, and researcher. He was an award-winning investigative journalist as senior staff writer at Shore Publishing in Madison, Connecticut, in 2006 and 2008. His articles and features have seen print in a wide variety of publications, including *Sailing* magazine, *Air Beat* magazine, *Atlantic Coast Fisheries News*, and the *Block Island Times*. Rayner is executive director of Water Emergency Training, Inc., a nonprofit organization dedicated to saving lives through drowning-prevention education and training.

Contents

Acknowledgments

I would like to thank my editor on this manuscript, Marisa Nadolny. Marisa's expertise and knowledge have been invaluable on this and several other projects. However, any errors are mine and mine alone.

Introduction

My passion is the water, and I've had that passion for as long as I've had memories. I learned to swim on Long Island Sound and the rivers and creeks that feed it. I learned to surf and ride waves on the Rhode Island shore, and five decades later I am still flopping around in the surf. Like many who grow up on the water, I actively fish, surf, boat, paddle, scuba dive, and darn near everything else you can do in or on it. I have been lucky enough to have traveled to some exotic destinations, from Michigan to South America, and my fascination and respect of the water has never ebbed.

I like to think I am a beach advocate, and I encourage everyone to take advantage of our waterways, learn to swim, and get wet, whether it's in a backyard pool or on a stretch of remote coastline. But this precious, ubiquitous liquid, essential for human existence, is, unfortunately, sometimes deadly. Fueled by my love of the water, I have made it my life goal to try to prevent these needless tragedies.

The statistics are sobering. According to the Centers for Disease Control, drowning is the leading cause of accidental death in children under fourteen years of age, and it also ranks among the top causes of death for young men in their teens and twenties.

When a life is lost to accident—vehicle, aircraft, drowning—there is a ripple effect that can last for generations. Children are never born; sons, daughters, nieces, nephews, and grandkids never come into the world as the result of a brief, seemingly innocuous decision. In this book you will learn how to prevent the emergency and, if that fails, how to survive by utilizing both your mind and body to gain an edge over Mother Nature. In my previous job as a survival instructor, I learned a great deal about safety, risk, and human psychology. I began intensive research into how people learn and how they retain knowledge, and believe me—there are enough theories out there to fill a library with books on the subject.

As a result, I strived to focus this guide yet still make it accessible to the novice and experienced adventurers. The goal is to inform across all levels of water experience, from the single mom who wants a little confidence when she takes her kids to the beach, to the experienced navigator who has already faced water emergencies. My hope is that everyone will take away a better appreciation of the environment and its dangers, as well as a set of skills they can implement in an emergency.

So what happens when you fall into fifty-degree water and you can't get out?

What do you do?

Unfortunately, even if you know how to swim, even if you have water experience, your survival time in temperatures below fifty-five degrees Fahrenheit is not measured in hours or even minutes; it's often measured in seconds. In fact, a majority of drownings occur in less than a minute! Victims can be actively drowning in less than thirty seconds. Regardless of the water temperature, a significant percentage of drowning victims perish fewer than six feet from shore, a dock, or other structure.[1]

Roughly 3,500 people drown every year in the United States, and many of these deaths could have been prevented.[2] I have had the sad experience of being on scene at several drownings, so I know firsthand how devastating these tragedies can be. It is a misconception that drowning victims scream, splash, and cry for help. Most victims slip below the surface unheard and undetected by anyone. Every day in this country, people drown within an arm's length of another person. That may sound unbelievable, but it is an absolute fact.

I want to emphasize that.

I have studied real-life films and witnessed real drownings and near-drownings, and counter to common sense, victims usually slip below the surface without a sound, often drowning within feet of parents or other adults. (See *On Drowning* by Water Safety Films, Inc. Compiled by Frank Pia, a former lifeguard and water-safety expert, the film shows footage of Long Island beaches in the 1970s and 1980s that demonstrates this phenomenon.)[3]

In 2011, a mother of two drowned at a YMCA pool in Fall River, Massachusetts. This tragedy gained national attention because, sadly, her body was not discovered for several days. Lost in the headlines was the fact that there was security video of this tragedy. The victim came down a waterslide, briefly surfaced, and then disappeared. Two lifeguards and dozens of people were within close proximity, and no one noticed because there were no screams, no splashing, and no cries.[4]

I have trained countless clients from across the aviation and marine industries, and I have interviewed numerous survivors. Many of these survivors possessed vast experience, spending more time on the water in a week than most do in a year, yet they still found themselves, despite their knowledge and background, at the mercy of the environment. Again and again I have come across very skilled and very experienced watermen (and women) whose training did not prepare them for avoiding a water emergency or for surviving one.

In my interviews with these survivors, those who spent months battling the water and those who spent only minutes, the overarching emotion they express is always humility. They speak of a profound gratitude for surviving but also of a deep humbleness born of gazing upon the uncaring face of Mother Nature.

So why all the gloom and doom?

I say this to shock you into focus because I know from personal experience that there is no more debilitating or frightening event than to be in trouble in the water with no one to help you. The physical and mental impact can kill even the hardiest and most experienced waterman very quickly. The decisions you make in the first few seconds can determine your fate.

The good news is that you can survive. There are very basic and simple procedures you can adopt that will lower your chances of facing an emergency and will increase your chances of survival if you do.

The information in this guide will allow you gain that knowledge and, hopefully, avoid the emergency altogether. The easiest way to survive an emergency is to never face one. However, even the most skilled and highly trained person can find himself or herself in a life-or-death emergency, so you need to know what to do if you do find yourself alone in the water.

Prevention

Avoiding an emergency is the simplest way to stay alive.

The Seven Ps is a mnemonic used by the US military and some marketing firms: "Proper prior planning and preparation prevents poor performance."

Preparation is the key word of this advice, and even the slightest amount of planning can prevent an emergency. There are two main thrusts of prevention: one is your personal thinking mechanism, and the other is the groupthink.

To prevent an emergency, reflect on your personal skills and detriments. If you can bench-press four hundred pounds but you can't swim, is it really a good idea to try to make it to the raft moored forty yards away? Know your limitations. Do not be embarrassed by them; own them. Being wary of the water because you can't swim doesn't mean you're a wimp; it means you are smart.

Know your limitations.

I understand how hard it is to follow this rule. As a lifelong surfer, there was a time when nothing charged me up more than big surf, and it forged a deep connection for me to the ocean. But these days, gone is the thrill because I know that I am simply too old to paddle out on certain swells. Know when to say when.

If you're the best captain on the seas, you train, you know your equipment, you take all safety precautions, you follow the rules, and you keep your arrogance in check; all of those factors become useless if you are the one who is unconscious or incapacitated during the emergency. Don't be lulled into risky behavior just because you know the water. Does everyone on the boat or in the water have the same level of confidence? Every person who steps on your vessel, jumps in your pool, or fishes off your dock should know basic water safety. Everyone should know how life vests operate and where they're located. Everyone near the water, experienced or novice, should know basic water common sense and safety. Everyone should know and master the techniques described in this book.

A recent positive example from my own observation came while working near a local boat launch. I watched an obviously inexperienced boater and his "helper" struggle to launch, tie off, and manage their small Whaler at the dock. It was not a good boating day for expert or novice. A very thick fog was hanging onto Long Island Sound, and visibility was barely fifty feet. Eventually, the vessel got under way, and I shook my head as the boat disappeared into the grayness, knowing no boater should've been on the water in those conditions. However, much to my surprise, they returned barely ten minutes later, trailered the boat, and left.

Great call, and very simple to do.

No fish, no trip, no fun is worth a life. Simply having the fortitude to make a decision such as that is incredibly important to survival.

Know how your equipment operates.

You won't be able to decipher the nuances of a life vest or life raft in the throes of an emergency. The time to find out the subtle manipulation of tension straps or the manual inflation of your life vest isn't after you've gone in the water.

Arrogance and complacency are the biggest causes of many water emergencies.

Most people don't describe themselves as arrogant, yet those very same people leave the dock blissfully ignorant of how foolhardy their behavior is. Many mariners don't even know where the marine band emergency channel on their radio is located and wouldn't be able to broadcast their position, even if they did.

Every weekend of the Northeast's boating season I shake my head incredulously when I am out on the water and see example after example of intelligent people who are simply unaware of the danger they are putting themselves in, from a sixty-year-old woman by herself, a half-mile from shore on a kayak, with no life vest; to ten bow-riding children without vests on an overloaded boat. Then there are the weekend warriors with no license or training and experienced boaters who know the rules but knowingly disregard them because "that stuff happens to other people." Add to that the legion of booze- and drug-addled mariners, and it can lead to a tragic outcome.

Many of the survivors I have interviewed made statements such as, "I should've checked," "I thought I heard something funny," "I knew the conditions were bad, but …" At these critical junctures don't be hesitant to make that call. Disappointed passengers are a small price to pay for safety.

Arrogance and water do not mix.

Complacency and water do not mix.

I can offer a very sad example from my own life. I spent more than a decade surfing and scuba diving the Great Lakes. (Despite its inland position, there are some great waves on the lakes.) One afternoon many years ago, friends and I were surfing one of our favorite spots at a small Michigan beach town along its namesake lake. The surf was actually quite big, and it was a great day, made even better when my friends rescued an intoxicated man from the water. They pulled him out of the waves and brought him safely back to shore. There was little drama—no CPR or mouth-to-mouth—but a lifesaving act nonetheless.

However, just minutes after we left the beach, witnesses stated that this individual reentered the water and drowned. In this case, alcohol undoubtedly played a factor and cost this person his life. Unfortunately, decisions like these are made every day.

Listen to your inner voice of caution, and don't be afraid to speak up.

This is just as important in a group setting. When it comes to groupthink or the crowd mentality, do not be embarrassed to go against the grain. According to various case studies and research, humans are very hesitant to act against the group. In 1969, authors and researchers Bibb Latane and Judith Rodin conducted what is referred to as the Lady in Distress experiment. In this study, test subjects were manipulated into believing that, just out of their sight, a researcher had fallen off a chair and presumably had been injured. When other people were present, only 7 percent responded to the "emergency." Seven percent! When alone, almost 70 percent of the test subjects reacted and helped in some way. That's a tenfold difference! When smoke was used as the motivating factor in an alternate version of this experiment, 75 percent of those who were alone reported it, and only 38 percent reported it when in a group. Can you imagine sitting in your seat and not reacting to smoke pouring into a room? Yet more than 60 percent of us do just that![1]

Why?

The conclusion of the authors was "Basically, these experiments show there are strong situational factors that can inhibit people from acting in emergencies."[2]

Humans are simply reluctant to go against the group, regardless of the scenario. Don't roll along with the herd when you suspect something is amiss. Don't be embarrassed to speak up.

If you have to ask the question “Is it safe?” “Is it too far?” or “What was that noise?” it’s probably not safe, it is too far, and you need to check that noise.

Avoid the emergency!

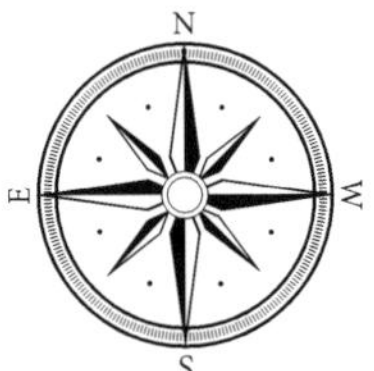

Pool Safety

Where do you think your child is safer—in a home where there is a pool or where there is a loaded firearm?

Most parents would probably choose the former, obviously perceiving that a firearm is far more likely to kill or maim their children. However, CDC statistics clearly demonstrate that a child is ten times more likely to drown in a pool or hot tub than to be accidently shot with a firearm.[1]

With that in mind, it makes sense to learn how you can prevent drownings in your home or anywhere children come into contact with water. It takes only inches of water to drown a human. A child, especially an infant, can drown in a five-gallon bucket with very little water in it.

Drowning is among the leading causes of injury-related death for children under fourteen years of age. Drowning is also a primary cause of accidental death for individuals between the ages of fifteen and twenty-five, especially males, according to CDC and National Safety Council data from 2001. Roughly ten people a day drown in the United States. Every year, approximately 1.2 million people drown worldwide.[2]

According to these same CDC annual reports, the consequences of near-drowning are devastating. As many as 20 percent of near-drowning survivors suffer severe and permanent neurological disabilities post-incident. The treatments also can take a tremendous financial toll. Typical medical costs for a near-drowning victim can range from $75,000 to $180,000 a year for long-term care. An incident involving brain injury can cost upwards of $4.5 million.[3]

Though pool design and construction have been a determining factor in many home drowning incidents, recent improvements and legislation have curbed these as causes. The number-one cause of home drowning continues to be *inattention* by supervising adults. It is important to emphasize that drowning most often occurs without warning. There is no splashing or yelling by the victim, especially children. Only brief moments of inattention or lack of supervision lead to drowning tragedies.

Don't allow safety devices to make you complacent.

This section will cover numerous safety devices and how they can save lives, but don't let your guard down. There is a phenomenon called *risk homeostasis* that factors into some of these tragedies.[4] (This is a debated theory in safety management with polar-opposite conclusions. I cite it here to reflect the well-established phenomenon of complacency and how it factors into emergencies.) It is quite common that upon the advent or implementation of a safety device, injuries and fatalities actually increase. Some examples: car seat belts, windshield wipers, and antilock brakes. When these devices were first introduced, accidents actually increased as a result. The same holds true for skydiving. Despite safety improvements and technological upgrades, skydiving deaths hold constant.

Why?

People thought they could take more risks because they had a safety device to save them. "I have a seat belt; therefore, I can drive faster [longer; in worse conditions]." Do not fall into this trap. Any safety device is only as good as its weakest link. (The good news on risk homeostasis is that data seem to indicate that eventually, when use of such devices becomes widespread, they perform as intended, and injury/fatality rates drop.)

Drowning-Prevention Equipment

Make sure every aspect of your safety equipment and plan is implemented according to its design and is in proper working order when it comes to your pool or hot tub. This holds true for anywhere you recreate in water, whether as an owner or visitor.

Fencing

Proper fencing around a pool is required by law in the United States. Make sure that fencing, especially on a residence that has an existing pool, is up to code and functioning correctly. (I have friends who bought a house with a pool in the mid-2000s that had subcode fencing, which a home inspection had missed. Don't assume the existing fencing is adequate.) Hot tubs have fewer requirements and codes, but they still need to have proper barriers and/or locks. A fence or lock is only safe if it is working properly. Broken mechanisms are a hidden danger and a tragedy waiting to happen.

Alarms

All doors from the residence into or onto the pool area should have an alarm. A surface disruption alarm also should be installed. These devices sound an alarm if the surface is disturbed, such as a child or pet falling in. They are usually removed during supervised swimming and replaced on the surface when the pool is not monitored.

However, alarms must be present to provide protection. The device can only work if it is on. Don't get complacent with this or any alarm, and don't suffer from false-alarm fatigue. Just like a car alarm that no one pays attention to, if the device constantly sounds, you may not react in a true emergency.

Pool Covers

Some pool covers are designed to prevent accidental falls into the water, but most do not. If you use a pool cover for safety, make sure it is designed for this purpose. Pool covers designed for thermal or maintenance protection do not provide protection from drowning. They can actually create hazards by entangling individuals who have fallen into the water.

Pool Nets

Recent safety innovations include pool nets, which are specifically designed to prevent drowning by keeping victims clear of the water surface. They are easily installed and removed and are specifically intended for safety purposes only. (Nets are also a good idea to prevent pet and wildlife drownings as well. Frogs, toads, snakes, and numerous species of rodents all find their way into pools.)

Cameras

Cameras are an excellent addition to a pool safety plan, but they cannot be relied on for primary safety for the home pool. They should be used as an enhancement system for home/public pool and hot tub safety. Inattention with a camera system is just as dangerous as inattention without it.

Hot Tub Safety

Temperature

Though not often associated with drowning, the temperature of a hot tub can often be set too high for small children. Read and follow manufacturer recommendations for your brand and style of hot tub.

Covers

Every hot tub should come with a securely locking cover. Make sure your cover functions properly and, most important, is in place whenever the tub is not in use. As with any other safety device, if it is not installed or in use, it is useless as a safety mechanism.

Supervision

The leading cause of drowning in children is lack of adult supervision.[5]

Parents and caretakers cannot be too safe when it comes to this practice. Children must be under constant watch by an adult who is physically and mentally equipped to deal with emergencies and capable of a rapid response. Drownings occur quickly. Remember: drowning victims usually do not splash, shout, or yell for help. If you are in charge, especially in this connected age, put your phone down and pay attention. Don't rely on other children or swimmers to initiate a rescue or even recognize the emergency. Numerous videos and films have documented children actively drowning or in distress while standing right next to friends and family. It is sobering to watch many of these videos as bystanders remain completely unaware of the crisis just feet from them.

Pool Rules

Create, implement, and adhere to a set of safety rules for your pool. These can vary, depending on the size and shape of your pool and whether you have a diving board. Once set, the pool rules should be followed consistently by any person using your pool or hot tub.

Swimming Lessons

Teaching young children to swim is an essential part of any home water-safety plan, but it cannot be the sole focus of drowning prevention. Many adults seek to "drown-proof" children with swimming lessons. This is not possible. Though swimming skills are essential to overall safety and are recommended for any child, it can also lead to a false sense of security for parents and students. Teach your children to swim, but do not rely on that skill alone to prevent water-based emergencies.

Emergency Drills

Be certain that any child using your pool, even a one-time guest, knows the pool rules and where safety devices are located. Is the thirteen-year-old babysitter physically able to pull a child, especially a panicked or incapacitated child, from your home pool or hot tub? Can a grandparent charged with watching a child realistically dive to the bottom of the deep end and remove a child from the water?

Kids these days are smart enough to dial 911, but that's not enough to save lives. Any child who uses your pool also should be practiced in pool safety and emergency drills. The first neighborhood pool party of the season is a great opportunity for all to learn how difficult water extraction can be. Make emergency drills fun. A game of Marco Polo that hones in on a floating child making the calls can be valuable. Have children locate "Marco Polo" on his/her back and then take the person safely to an egress point. This can provide invaluable insight and knowledge to even young children.

Extraction of an Unconscious Victim in the Water

This recommendation is for a victim without a suspected spinal injury. If there is any possibility of a spinal injury, allow medical professionals to perform any extraction or treatment. Backyard aboveground pools do not have graduated bottoms that allow for a rescuer to easily pull a victim from the water. Pulling a hundred-pound teenager the one foot from the surface of the water to the deck is difficult. Do you jump in and lift the victim up? Do you pull the victim from the water up to the deck?

Remember, anyone watching children around water should be able to perform an extraction. For years at my former job as a water-safety instructor, we tested and tried to develop pool-extraction techniques that were practical. Quite frankly, we never came to a consensus on the best way to get an unconscious person from the water surface onto the deck of a pool without a backboard. The best option is an extraction board, but no pool owner can be expected to purchase and store this device. As stated, I have seen and participated in many styles of extraction. My recommendation, especially if you're by yourself, is a towel extraction. It's not ideal, but when performed properly it will allow a smaller person to extract a larger person from the water.

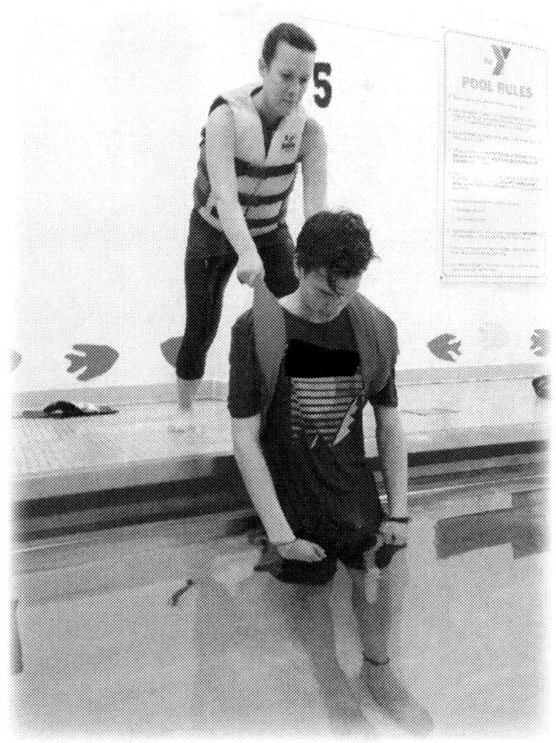

Towel Extraction

Photo: Ben Rayner

This photo demonstrates the towel extraction technique. This can be employed when water level prevents an easy removal of an unconscious person from the water. Simply get a towel, twist it tightly, and then loop it under both armpits of the victim across his or her back. Pull the ends over the top of the arms and the towel becomes an effective gripping device to drag a person up onto a deck or platform. This technique is not foolproof, but it can aid in difficult extractions.

Unfortunately, there are numerous cases of home pool tragedies where the supervising adult did not know how to swim and stood by helplessly as victims needlessly drowned. A person who supervises children should be able to perform some basic lifesaving techniques. Calling 911 is not enough.

Flotation Devices

There is a significant distinction between life vests or life preservers and floatation devices. Flotation devices are toys, and though they can be effective in emergency situations, they should not be used as the primary lifesaving device. Supervising adults should be certain that children, especially those without swimming skills, are wearing life vests at all times and that they are donned correctly. Vests can be an essential component of water safety, but as with other devices, life vests cannot be relied on to drown-proof individuals of any age. (Refer to chapter 5 for a full description of life vests.)

Diving Boards

Diving boards were traditionally a cause of injury and drowning in home pools. Recent design changes and updated codes and regulations for diving boards have lessened the danger, but these devices continue to be a hazard. My recommendation is that homeowners not include a diving board in their pool design and remove an existing board if purchasing a home with a pool.

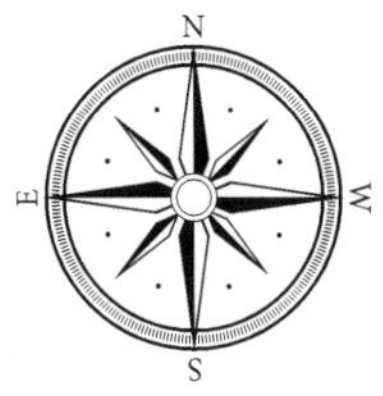

Hypothermia Mitigation and Cold-Water Immersion

According to oceanologists, the average worldwide ocean temperature ranges between fifty and sixty degrees Fahrenheit. Water below sixty degrees is designated as "cold water."[1] When humans are immersed in these temperatures, their survival time is not measured in hours or even minutes but often in seconds. Preparation and mastery of simple skills can greatly increase your odds of survival in any water emergency.

To begin, in technical terms, very few people involved in water emergencies actually die from hypothermia. That sounds counterintuitive, but it is a much-researched fact of exposure.[2]

Hypothermia is a drop in the body's core temperature, and that is a function of temperature and time. Most drowning victims, in cold or cool water, are dead long before hypothermia sets in or can be clinically diagnosed.

This phenomenon is referred to as *cold shock* and has been recognized by researchers in only the last few decades. One incident in particular underscores how scientists began to look more closely at how and why people perish long before hypothermia can develop.

In February 1990, a group of at-risk teens and their mentors were on a nature hike at Convict Lake in the Sierra Nevada Mountains of California. Several of the boys ventured out onto the ice and fell through. Then several of the adult leaders attempted to rescue them, and they broke through the ice as well. Help was summoned quickly, and rescue professionals, including a member of the US Forest Service and two volunteer firefighters, arrived on scene. However, they also broke through the ice and, tragically, three children and four of the five adult rescuers drowned in less than fifteen minutes.[3]

When better-equipped emergency personnel eventually effected the rescue, the lone surviving adult was hyperventilating uncontrollably, panicking, and very close to drowning. However, none of these victims died from hypothermia; in fact, according to the investigating medical professionals, the survivor's body temperature was normothermic (meaning a normal body core temp).[4]

So what actually occurs when someone enters cold water?

Two distinct hazards of cold water will affect both physical and mental function in humans. The first, called *cold-water immersion*, is instantaneous, and the symptoms rapidly lead to drowning. A significant percentage of people, even those with swimming skills and water experience, can begin actively drowning in a matter of moments due to cold-water immersion. The impairment of mental and physiological functions is so intense that it is critical to be prepared and act quickly in water emergencies.

The second cold-water hazard is *hypothermia*. This is a quantifiable drop in the core body temperature and develops over a period of time. This condition leads to cardiac arrest, cerebral hemorrhage, and a number of other nasty ways to perish.

Cold-Water Immersion

The first and most critical stage of cold-water immersion is called the *cold-water gasp reflex*. When thrust into cold water, a human will gasp uncontrollably, leading to airway compromise and the aspiration of water. This is an involuntary physiological phenomenon. Even on a calm water surface, this condition is extremely hazardous and is a major contributor of drownings in cooler water. Keeping control of your breath is vital. Victims also can begin to hyperventilate at this stage in an attempt to catch their breath, which can increase panic and compound their inability to breathe. People have drowned at the surface of the water while wearing a life vest due to the gasp reflex. Even a small wave state or sea spray can cause people to aspirate water and drown.[5]

What to Do

In the midst of the gasp reflex, hold your breath, and try to keep from gasping for as long an interval as you can. This is difficult to accomplish and can be managed for only a few seconds, as the symptoms will continue to recur. However, if you maintain holding your breath for these short durations, the effects of the gasp reflex will slowly begin to ebb. Do not try to perform any other skills or maneuvers until your breathing is under control. This can take a minute or longer.

I have suffered this phenomenon, and it is very debilitating. The fear is intensified because you are so close to the water and cannot catch your breath. There is evidence that some level of inoculation or acclimatization to the gasp reflex is possible with repeated immersions. When I surf during the winter, the gasp reflex tends to lessen in frequency and intensity the more I am in the water, but there is no standard by which to measure this. I have suffered the gasp reflex in June in sixty-five-degree water.

The Mammalian Dive Reflex

The second stage of cold-water immersion is called the *mammalian dive reflex,* and it also has a rapid onset. When the body cools, capillaries are constricted as blood is drawn from the extremities and shunted to the core. This restricted blood flow makes the ability to use one's hands and feet progressively more difficult. If the gasp reflex is occurring, even an experienced, physically fit individual can lose muscle control quickly and drown. Fine dexterity falters rapidly, and simple tasks—like pulling the toggle of a life vest, manipulating a manual inflation tube, or grasping a lifeline—become impossible.[6]

Case histories of survivors reveal people so affected by cold-water immersion that they could not grab onto lifelines or pull themselves into rafts. Survivors have reported hands so numb that once inside, they couldn't open the thick vacuum packaging of safety items in their survival kits. (Refer to chapter 7 for more on the testimony of Paul Blarney. He was among a handful of survivors of the *Estonia* sinking in the Baltic Sea in 1996, with the loss of close to one thousand souls.)[7]

Swimming Failure

The next stage of cold-water immersion is swimming failure. This is also a function of time and heat loss, but swim failure can develop quickly. This can occur before or during clinical hypothermia. The restriction in blood flow from the dive reflex starves the larger muscle groups, weakening the victim. The inability to swim or manipulate appendages leads to drowning; in some recorded cases, it occurred very quickly.[8]

Hypothermia Fast Facts

- Humans lose body heat twenty-four to twenty-five times faster in water than in air.[9]

- Hypothermia is the condition in which the core body temperature drops below the threshold required for normal metabolism, which is 95 degrees F (35 degrees C).[10]

- It is a myth that you lose more heat from your head than the rest of your body. (The mistake is based on some erroneous conclusions reached by dated US Army testing.)[11] It's still a good idea to wear a hat, but you lose heat anywhere on your body that is exposed to the air or water.

- Several recorded body temperatures of hypothermia victims have been in the mid-50s F. A seven-year-old female survived a recorded core temperature of 55.4 degrees F after a drowning incident in Sweden in December 2010. According to medical studies, many hypothermia victims with body core temps below eighty don't survive. These extreme cases are the exception rather than the rule. Every year, dozens—perhaps hundreds—of victims in the United States alone, most with water experience and swimming skills, rapidly perish due to cold-water immersion.[12]

Mild Hypothermia Symptoms

99–96 degrees F: Uncontrollable shivering is the first sign of hypothermia.

95–91 degrees: Violent shivering progresses; mental confusion and slurred speech develops.

Moderate Hypothermia Symptoms

90–86 degrees: Shivering decreases as the body loses energy; muscular rigidity develops; mental confusion becomes more pronounced.

85–81 degrees: Pulse and respiration slows.

Severe Hypothermia Symptoms

80–78 degrees: Unconsciousness occurs; cessation of reflexes and an erratic heartbeat develops.

Below 78 degrees: Irregular heartbeat, cardiac arrest, and death occurs.[13]

(Some scales include a fourth or profound stage below 68 degrees F.)

The actual onset of clinical hypothermia is difficult to determine, especially for those without medical training. Each victim is different, and each scenario can have many variants.

Don't be misinformed by the term "mild" or "moderate." Hypothermia is serious in all stages, not just the severe stage. The effects of even mild hypothermia, especially combined with those of cold-water immersion, can be lethal. A simple symptom like involuntary shivering can be so intense that gripping is impossible, preventing victims from helping themselves or others.

Another complication of hypothermia is something most people would find strange. This stage is called *after-drop* or *post-rescue collapse*, and in some cases it can be fatal. There are several ways in which this effect can manifest in victims. According to some statistics, 20 percent of people pulled from the water undergo as much as an eight-degree drop in body core temperature after being rescued.[14] That doesn't seem to be logical, but this phenomenon has been recorded since the earliest tales of sea survival, going back to ancient Phoenician and Greek mariners.

Strangely enough, medical treatment of hypothermia victims can be life-threatening. A victim with severe hypothermia who is aggressively rewarmed can go into shock and die for several reasons. As the body sends blood back to the extremities from the core, a dangerous decrease in blood pressure can initiate cardiac arrest and even a stroke. The effects of hypothermia also can cause acidosis, a buildup of acid in the muscle tissues. When this chemical is released by intense rewarming, it can cause cardiac and cerebral events.[15]

What to Do

The prevailing medical wisdom is that anyone with a core body temperature above ninety degrees should be *actively rewarmed*, and those below ninety degrees should be *passively rewarmed.*

Active rewarming techniques include rubbing body parts, alcohol rubs, and forceful heating. It is critical, however, not to attempt any active techniques if there is a possibility of severe hypothermia. Increased handling or movement of a severely hypothermic victim increases the risk for heart dysrhythmia, stroke, and blood pressure imbalances. If warming a victim with water, use warm water, not hot. Also, monitor the person as he or she can easily lapse into a number of critical conditions.

Passive rewarming techniques include removing wet clothing, laying a victim on his or her side, covering with a blanket or warm fabric, and sharing body heat.[16]

I normally don't carry a rectal thermometer as part of my safety kit, so it is difficult to verify the core temperature of a hypothermia victim. As such, emergency medical personnel recommend assuming a person is in a critical stage and to passively rewarm only.

I have basic medical training, and from experience I know it can be very difficult to assess any patient's symptoms. However, one way to determine the severity of hypothermia is by engaging victims in conversation. If they can converse cogently, more than likely they have mild or moderate hypothermia. If they weave in and out of conversation, have heavily slurred speech, or profound mental impairment, assume it is severe hypothermia.

The most effective treatment you can initiate for a water-based hypothermia victim is to remove wet clothing. Victims are better off standing naked, exposed to the air, than they are in wet clothes.

Next, if the victim is conscious and alert, try to get glucose or sugar into him or her. A candy bar or the food items of a life raft survival kit are recommended to restore the energy reserves of a person with hypothermia. Never put any food or liquid into the mouth of an unconscious person, regardless of the emergency.

Post-rescue collapse also can be caused by a significant drop in blood pressure. When victims are pulled from the water, especially after extended periods, they can suffer a massive decrease in blood pressure, which can lead to death. This is because the body has been countering the water weight on it. Once the pressure is alleviated by rescue, the circulatory system slows, and the blood pressure falls quickly and dramatically.[17]

In general it is best to keep victims lying prone on one side. Provide glucose/sugar if possible, share body heat, get them dry, and slowly rewarm them.[18]

As the length of immersion progresses, hypothermia begins to affect the mind as well as the body. On a personal note, I have suffered cold-water immersion and mild to moderate hypothermia on more than one occasion. I have endured many of the classic effects and can testify that the loss of mind and body function can be quite profound.

(For more on this topic, please read *Hypothermia, Frostbite, and Other Cold Injuries* by Gordon Giesbrecht, PhD, and James A. Wilkerson, PhD. Giesbrecht is known as Professor Popsicle for his research into cold injuries. He is perhaps the most knowledgeable authority on this topic, and his data continues to be at the forefront of all water-safety recommendations. Their book contains a wealth of experimental data and is considered by many in the survival industry as the go-to source on the subject of hypothermia.)

I also have experienced another phenomenon called *cold-induced vasodilation (CIVD)*, which compounds the hazard of hypothermia and compromises survival. Though the scientific community does not completely understand the exact mechanism, many hypothermia victims suffer CIVD when the constricted vessels of the extremities open up, and a rapid flush of warm blood begins to circulate through the system. (Remember: the body has shunted blood flow to your trunk and torso during the mammalian dive reflex. Some experts believe the body just gets tired and is forced by energy loss to disengage from the dive reflex, but exactly how this works in the human body is not well defined.)

The feeling can be so intense that victims feel quite warm and relaxed, as if they are getting a second wind. Survivors tell of actually sweating as they are perishing from hypothermia.

CIVD is extremely dangerous, as it can lead to another fatal condition called *paradoxical undressing.*[19] According to published medical sources, this affects somewhere between 20 to 50 percent of hypothermia victims. Some hypothermia fatalities have been found stark naked within reach of heat-generating materials, but they are so affected by CIVD that they strip off all protective clothing. The removal of clothes obviously compounds their hypothermia, making survival even more unlikely.

Perhaps the most alarming aspect of CIVD, in my experiences, is that I did not feel disoriented or mentally impaired in any way. I had no hint that I was suffering a loss of acuity or any physical detriment. I felt hyperalert and in possession of my faculties, despite the fact that I was removing vital components of my wetsuit in thirty-four-degree water. The entire time that I was relishing my second wind and my ability to conquer Mother Nature, I was succumbing to hypothermia.

Think 1–10–1

Another useful rubric is the 1–10–1 formula. This theory states that in fifty-five-degree water or less, in general, you have about one minute to get your breathing under control, about ten minutes of useful movement time, and about one hour to live. There are numerous factors that can lessen or increase these numbers but they are a baseline from which to get a grasp of how quickly victims are overcome by the environment.[20]

Keep in mind many people are actively drowning within seconds of going into the water, so these numbers are of little use in those situations.

Preventing immersion is the only guaranteed method of avoiding the effects of hypothermia, but what do you do if you have fallen off the dock in early March without a life vest, or a line has pulled you off the stern at three in the morning?

The HELP Position

Always wear a life vest and know how to use it.

A life vest will save your life in several different ways. It will help to stave off hypothermia because its flotation will minimize your movement and save body energy. There are numerous styles and brands of life vests, and all have different features and deployment systems. Don't rely on a water-activated hydrostatic vest to automatically deploy as designed. Know how to use the manual inflation system of your vest. If you are unsure of how your vest works, open it up and read any directions and the manual. The opportunity to understand how your vest works is when you are high and dry, not in the midst of an emergency.

The vest is donned. Now what?

There are also a few simple techniques that can assist in individual and group hypothermia mitigation. The technique that works best for individual hypothermia mitigation is the *heat escape lessening posture (HELP)* position. The HELP position may be the single most important survival skill to master if you find yourself in a water emergency.

The technique is characterized by adopting the fetal position to lessen heat loss. Grab the front or back of your knees and hug them with moderate force. (This cannot be accomplished effectively without a life vest or flotation aid.) Don't squeeze too strongly; that is exhausting and will waste precious calories. A moderate grip is sufficient. Once you have a good grasp, simply lean your head back and go with the flow. The HELP position minimizes water flow across the body, which lessens heat loss to the environment and provides a valuable extension of survival time.

Enhancing this technique with a simple trash bag will save your life.

A three-mil contractor's-grade trash bag can be slipped on over the feet and works like a poor man's wetsuit. Instead of heating the whole ocean, your body warms only the water in the bag. Trash bags are lightweight, take up little room, and can be stowed easily in or on a life vest. Many brands of vests have pockets that will accommodate a large bag. If yours doesn't, use rubber bands or zip ties to secure a bag to your vest.

Get entirely inside the bag, including arms, elbows, and the lower lobes of the life vest, with just your head exposed. Even large people can accomplish this move. It is not a perfect solution; you will still lose heat to the water. However, because of the reduced surface area of skin exposed to the water, this technique can keep body core temperatures elevated far longer than other techniques or formations.

You cannot effectively move in the HELP position, but saving energy is the point. The less you move, the longer you will last. Minimizing movement also will keep water from sloshing in and out of the bag and wasting heat. Stay in the HELP position inside the bag and just go with the flow.

In general, the warmest part of the water column is usually the top foot. Depending on the body of water and the weather conditions, the difference in the temperature between the first foot of water and your feet can be more than five degrees Fahrenheit.[21] This is a critical amount. A one- or two-degree difference can mean life or death. This is why the HELP technique is so beneficial: It keeps the person in the warmest part of the water and minimizes movement.

Contractor's bags are most often black, restricting visibility to rescuers, so consider investing in a large three-mil Halloween pumpkin-style orange leaf bag. Keep in mind that once waves begin getting large, it can be impossible to remain in position to mitigate hypothermia, but the HELP has proven to save lives.

This tip may be the most important and easiest survival advice in this book. Bring a trash bag or two with you on any trip, land or water. Large bags can be repurposed for many uses and make very effective thermal barriers or shelters. Remember three-mil or thicker contractor's-grade bags are essential for this technique. Kitchen trash bags are too small and too thin.

HELP Position #1
Photo: Ben Rayner

Pictured here is a demonstration of the HELP position (heat escape lessening posture), both with and without the contractor's-bag enhancement. This is the recommended hypothermia mitigation technique if you go into the water alone. This technique is enhanced with the use of a contractor's-grade trash bag. Keep one in your life vest or survival kit. The "poor man's wetsuit" can keep you alive hours longer.

The Carpet Formation

If you are immersed with multiple survivors, the recommended group hypothermia mitigation technique is the carpet formation. The carpet formation allows the body core to float at the surface where the water is warmer. Survivors link arms with those on either side, and each interlocks his or her legs with the person across from him or her to share as much body heat as possible. (Give a right leg; take a right leg. See photo.) Grab the feet from the person in front of you and put that person's feet on your chest. To avoid wasting heat, don't let feet or legs dangle. (Dangling appendages may also attract marine life that you may not want to meet.)

There are a number of excellent benefits to this particular formation. The position is comfortable, energy is saved, and survivors can last far longer. Because there are so many points of contact, it keeps the group together, which raises morale. In fact, multiple members of the group can fall asleep or lose consciousness and still keep the formation together.

In this formation, no psychological energy needs to be expended wondering and worrying about where other people are in the water. The benefit of numbers assists in keeping the group calm, and the input of multiple ideas can be part of the survival strategy.

This formation also makes a larger target for rescuers to find. It is much easier to see three to five people huddled together, making a big blob on the surface, than to try to find five little heads poking above the waves, spreading away from each other.

The carpet formation allows for 360-degree skyward visibility, which means survivors can keep watch for rescue aircraft. Also, with even a small sea state, marine vessels can be observed as the waves pitch up and down.

It also creates a platform for an injured survivor or someone without a life vest to rest on. Though this person is not fully out of the water, he or she can be "floated" by the rest of the group.

The carpet is recommended above other group formations. There is an older US military technique called the "huddle" or "star" formation, in which survivors float vertically in the water, interlocking arms to form a big circle. However, this puts people in a position where the trunk of the body and legs are in a colder section of the water column, and body heat is not utilized. In the huddle, when just one person goes unconscious, the entire formation begins to break down and scatter survivors. Stick to the carpet, whether you have just two survivors or twenty. Just two people can face each other, interlock their legs, and extend their survival.

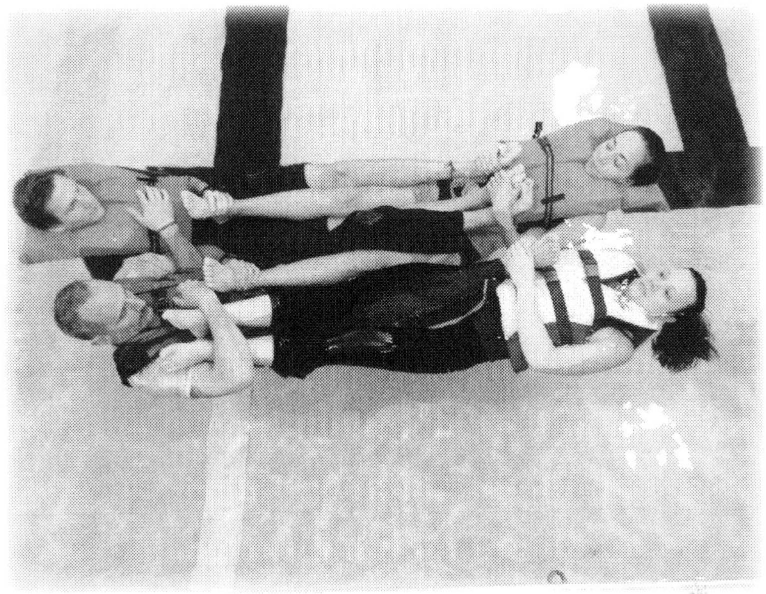

Carpet Formation

Photo: Ben Rayner

Above is a demonstration of the carpet formation. This is the most effective group hypothermia mitigation technique. There are numerous benefits to this formation, including the sharing of body heat, comfort, and general energy conservation.

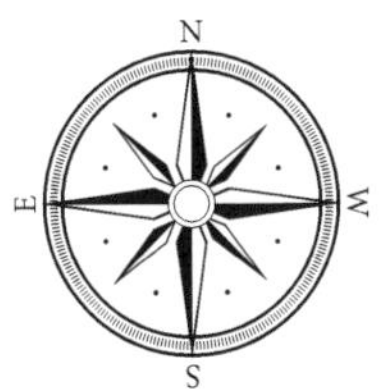

Life Vests and Immersion Suits

Note: Due to the specifics of United States Coast Guard regulations for life vests for both recreational and commercial use, it is not possible to fully cover all scenarios. This information should be used as a general guide. Consult the USCG required "Think Safe" pamphlet attached to your PFD in order to make the most informed choice concerning your specific activity.

Personal flotation devices (PFDs), life preserving units (LPUs), or whatever the name, for this chapter I will use the term from my generation: life vest or vest. If you don't know how one works or where it is, your chances for rescue from a water emergency drop significantly.

Vests are manufactured in a variety of styles and types. Each has specific criteria for classification and their intended use. Understanding not only the differences between types but also how they are worn can be a determining factor of survival.

According to United States Coast Guard (USCG) boating accident data, the advent and use of type III PFDs has reduced water fatalities in the last four decades significantly. While the number of people who engage in boating has steadily increased, the number of drownings while boating has decreased from about 1,500 annually in 1971 to 500 in 2006. According to the USCG, 1,286 people drowned for lack of a PFD in 1971; in 2006, 423 people drowned for lack of a PFD. This dramatic reduction occurred even though the number of boats increased from about 5.5 million to over 12 million during the same thirty-five-year period.[1]

That equates to roughly thirty-five thousand people who are alive due to use of life vests.

So why don't we wear them?

Comfort, looks, maneuverability—there are numerous reasons. But in light of the dramatic reduction in drownings by the use of vests, and keeping in mind your survival time in fifty- to sixty-degree water is dramatically short, there is no good argument against wearing a vest. However, even proper deployment doesn't guarantee survival. People drown at the surface while wearing a life vest, without their airways ever going underwater.

A life vest doesn't do much good if it is not properly donned. It seems like a no-brainer, but improper use of a vest can kill you. Once again, I must emphasize: know your equipment. Don't wait until you are in fifty-five-degree water, with a dislocated wrist, in ten-foot breaking seas to discover how your vest works.

Tips for Wearing a PFD Properly

Always don your life vest before assisting others. Tighten the device down so that it is snug to the torso. (You don't need to break ribs, but you should get darn close to that.) Almost all vests utilize waist straps. Most common civilian brands do not have "crotch" straps between the legs. Ensure that whatever style of straps are on your vest are cinched down and in the proper position. A loose vest can be even more lethal than no vest at all. Loose-fitting PFDs may not provide proper buoyancy and can fail to bring the user's airway above the surface. Improper use also can constrict an airway. Case histories have demonstrated that improperly fitted vests proved so uncomfortable that they were discarded by victims in the water, leading to fatalities.

PFDs (especially inflatables) can channel water between the lobes into the wearer's airway. Once the device is donned, wearers should face their backs to oncoming wind, waves, or swell. Take the swell over your back, not into your airway, especially if experiencing the gasp reflex.

Inherently buoyant vests are just that—buoyant. If properly donned there is no need to deploy the flotation mechanism by a gas charge or manually with breath. If the vest is an inflatable type and it fails to deploy, the wearer must manually inflate the lobes of the device by utilizing the oral inflation tubes. Inspect your vest and know how to deploy your manual system. Some are user-friendly and easy to use; others are complicated, and in the stress of an emergency they can be difficult to locate and fill.

Does your vest have pull tabs that use compressed gas for inflation? Where are the pull tabs located? (Some brands have frustratingly hard-to-find pulls.) Do they only have manual inflation? Knowing the answers to these questions before the emergency occurs can save vital seconds during the initial stages of an incident.

A PFD never should be deployed or donned inside an enclosed space. This will trap the user. In 1996 Ethiopian Airlines Flight 961 was hijacked and eventually crashed into the waters off the coast of East Africa in the Comoros Islands. Survivors stated that as the plane came in for the ditching after it ran out of fuel, the only sound was the inflation cylinders of the life vests going off. Many of the passengers survived the initial impact, but an estimated sixty to eighty of the victims perished as the result of drowning because they were trapped inside the wreckage by their vests. Pinned by the buoyancy of their vests, many victims died just feet from safety. This is also a hazard in marine emergencies if caught below deck on a vessel.[2]

A vest should not be deployed while underwater, unless the wearer is completely without air and struggling to surface. A PFD deployed underwater will force the wearer to make a rapid ascent, which could cause him or her to hit debris or other survivors, or to surface into fluids or fire that could cause injury.

During an emergency, never take your vest off, and never remove all of the air. It is permissible to let small quantities of air out in order to do physical acts, such as getting into a life raft or for comfort, but the device should never be taken off or have all of its air purged. The only circumstances in which it is recommended to release a small quantity of air are if movement is restricted, such as getting into a life raft or onto debris, or if hearing is restricted. Some vest designs, even when donned properly, can restrict hearing, hampering the ability to communicate with other survivors or to recognize rescue assets. Wave splash and precipitation can cause an echoing effect on inflatable PFDs.

Manual or oral inflation tubes, for the most part, operate in the same manner and are easy to use—once you find them. However, some designs require the wearer to screw up a neural nut for inflation. Certain brands have exceedingly difficult-to-access tubes. For example, in a dual-lobe system, if the top lobe of the vest is inflated first, it can make it impossible to get the tube of the bottom lobe to your mouth.

To adjust the fit of the vest, let small burps of air out. To accomplish this, most brands have a small valve to depress inside the top of the oral inflation tube. In most brands, only a pinky finger can get inside the tube, making it a delicate operation to depress the valve. It becomes even more difficult when compounded by cold shock, hypothermia, and the stress of an emergency. Don't get any water into the vest when performing this task. Valves depressed below the surface will allow water to flow back into the lobe. A small amount won't matter, but a larger volume could compromise flotation.

One Lobe or Two?

For many years I taught students in the military who were told by their training personnel to inflate only one lobe of their dual-lobe vest; in theory, this was to prevent both lobes from tearing or ripping. But there are a couple of flaws in that logic. One, a redundant lobe is only redundant if it's also inflated. If you're unconscious or otherwise incapacitated, you won't be able to fill the second lobe if the first is compromised. Also, whatever tears the top lobe is going to compromise the bottom lobe, whether it's inflated or not, so it might as well be filled.

Dual-lobe vests have added protection, but they also have a tendency to constrict the wearer's neck when inflated. As stated above, you can let air out to adjust the fit, but I have witnessed many students panic when vests inflated improperly or tightened around their necks.

One-lobe vests are effective. They are slimmer and less expensive but lack the redundancy of another tube.

The bottom line is to know your equipment.

Moving in a Vest

It is recommended that you swim on your back when wearing a life vest. Forward swimming strokes are cumbersome and use energy that your body needs to fend off hypothermia. There have been case histories of survivors removing life vests due to the frustration of their slow progress while swimming forward. Easy, lazy backstrokes are far more efficient in the water when wearing a vest of any type, and this strategy uses less energy and keeps the wearer in that warmest part of the water column. Also, try to keep your back to the prevailing sea state to avoid water into your face. As stated earlier, lobed vests can form a channel that can shove water into your airway.

In some situations it may be necessary or expedient to wear an inherently buoyant vest while below deck. Wearing any vest in an enclosed area for work or for sleep is a personal decision. If you decide to remove a vest for any reason, at the very least keep it in an easily accessible area so that it can be located in an emergency.

There are limitations to almost every life vest design. Inflatable PFDs have a number of limitations, as explained in the "Think Safe" pamphlet provided with them and, in some cases, as marked on them.

Additionally, the reliability of inflatable PFDs is less than that of inherently buoyant PFDs. The most frequent problem noted in studies is the required maintenance. While inflatable PFDs may increase use in some circumstances, they are not suitable for all water activities.

PFD Safety Checklist

Fit Your PFD

- Don your PFD to determine that it fits. It should be snug but also comfortable. Test your PFD in the water to establish that excessive ride-up does not impair its performance.

- Also test the buoyancy of your PFD in shallow water. If your PFD keeps your chin above water and is comfortable, it is a proper fit.
- Remember that swift water can change the way your life vest fits and supports you.

Wear Your PFD

- Most drownings do not occur offshore. According to the USCG, nine out of ten drownings occur in inland waters, most within a few feet of safety. A majority of the victims had access to PFDs but were not using them at the time of the incident.[3]
- Make sure all on board are wearing PFDs. Secure all straps, zippers, and ties to avoid getting entangled.
- Practice throwing type IV PFDs to improve accuracy. The USCG recommends tossing them underhand or side arm.

PFD Care and Maintenance

- Don't alter your PFD. An altered PFD may not function properly.
- Don't store heavy objects on your PFD or use it for a kneeling pad or boat fender. Some PFDs can lose buoyancy if this occurs. Don't store PFDs on a direct heat source, such as a radiator.
- Let your PFD drip-dry thoroughly, and stow it in a well-ventilated area of the vessel. (The charging cylinders of hydrostatic vests are prone to corrosion.)
- Periodically check your PFD for rips and holes, mildew, and shrinkage of materials. Seams, fabric straps, and hardware should all be free from rust and corrosion and in good working order.
- Don't forget to test every PFD at the start of each season. The USCG requires your PFDs be in serviceable condition

before you use your boat. Ones that do not pass inspection should be destroyed and disposed of properly.

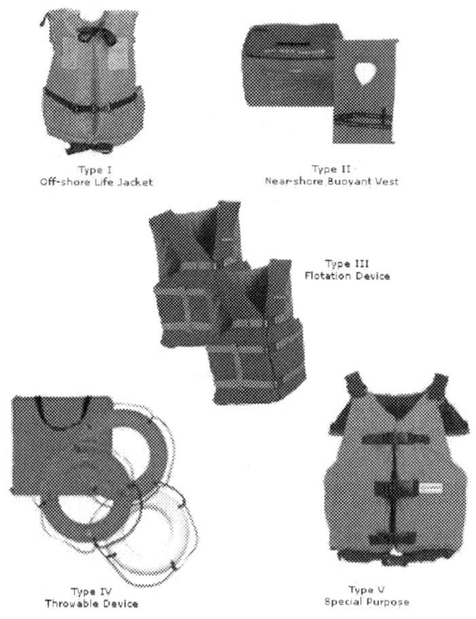

USCG Life Vests

Photo: Ben Rayner

All statistics cited in this chapter come from the 2009 and 2010 USCG fatality and accident reports. The recommendations come directly from the USCG "Think Safe" PFD manuals.

Immersion Suits

Immersion Suit

Immersion suits are fully encapsulating thermal protection PFDs that are most often used for commercial purposes. They come in various styles and brands. Note that some styles are not equipped with an inflatable headrest. Features of most suits include an inner thermal liner, open neck sealing, and other items such as mittens or gloves stowed in the sleeves and whistles tethered to the torso.

I do not recommend any manufacturer or style, but there are general overall features that users should consider:

- a whistle on a lanyard to permit the wearer to signal for help

- an emergency strobe light beacon with a water-activated battery
- an inflatable pillow/bladder to lift the wearer's head up out of the water
- tethered mittens to better insulate the hands
- an emergency radio locator beacon
- a "buddy line" to attach to others' suits to keep the group together for rescue
- sea dye markers to increase visibility in water

Open-Neck vs. Closed-Neck Sealing

A suit's method of sealing around the face and neck affects wearer comfort. Quick-donning suits typically have an open neck, closed by a water-resistant zipper. However, the zipper can be a stiffly functioning mechanism that tightly compresses around the face, resulting in an uncomfortable fit. Unlike work suits, quick-don survival suits are not normally worn but are stowed in an accessible onboard location. This style of suit is usually intended for short-duration use.

Suits designed for long-term work use or for rescue personnel typically have a form-fitting neck seal that greatly minimizes leakage. Most are equipped with a hood that conforms to the shape of the chin. This design is more comfortable and allows more freedom of movement and visibility.

However, suits with just a zipper and face shield are still very effective in keeping water out. Most manufacturers state that the suit will allow only a one-degree drop of body core temperature every hour in thirty-two degrees Fahrenheit water. Also, most suits are designed for (and factor in) leakage. Depending on the style and how and where it is donned, most testing is in consideration of up to one liter of water inside the suit. Water in the suit will lower comfort levels but does not affect the integrity of the suit or significantly alter survival times. According to manufacturers, an immersion suit extends a victim's survival time by many hours.

Fitting and Wearing an Immersion Suit

An adult survival suit is often a large, bulky, one-size-fits-all design, which can lead to improper fitting. If you invest in a suit or are issued one through an employer, take the time to ensure it is the correct size and is comfortable.

Suits typically have large, oversized booties and gloves built in, which let the user quickly don the suit while fully clothed and without having to remove shoes. Although if the emergency permits, shoes should be taken off for ease in donning.

Most brands have a waterproof zipper up the front and a face flap to keep water out around the neck and protect the wearer from ocean spray. Because of the oversized booties and large mittens, quick-don survival suits are often known as "Gumby suits," after the cartoon character.

There are two styles of gloves found on suits: integral and outer. If the suit has fitted integral gloves, they generally will be a thin, waterproof, noninsulated material that gives the user greater dexterity during donning and evacuation. These gloves are attached to the sleeve and are automatically donned when the user puts the suit on. Some manufacturers include a second insulating outer glove or mitten tethered in a pouch on the sleeves for additional protection. Some brands have both styles as part of their design, others only one.

A properly donned immersion suit is considered a PFD. An immersion suit that is not donned and deployed correctly will not provide protection to the user and, in some instances, will compound the hazard and lead to a fatality.

It is important to "burp" out excess air in the suit before entering the water, if possible. Open the neck seal slightly and kneel to allow air to be forced out through the neck opening. The face/head guard hoodie should go under the chin, and any face seal should go over the mouth. If too much air remains in the suit, it will make the device very uncomfortable and awkward to use. It could also be fatal. Air that is forced into the feet can invert the user. This is extremely dangerous and must be avoided.

If possible, try to slide into the water with as little motion as possible. Manufacturers recommend that wearers avoid jumping into the water with an immersion suit. Jumping into the water with a suit on, with or without excess air, can invert the feet and flip the wearer upside down. This pushes the user's airway under the water, making it very difficult to reright oneself.

The recommendation from the USCG is to don your suit in a pool or calm body of water, and make sure the suit fits and is comfortable. These suits are notoriously ill fitting, so "comfortable" is a relative term.

With a buddy or monitor, practice rerighting, getting your feet underneath you, as well as utilizing the features of the suit. If you enter the water and feel buoyancy at your feet, force them down into the water column, and break the neck seal to allow air to escape. Make sure all zippers are fully closed. Utilize the gloves/mitts if your suit is equipped with them. I have spent many hours in immersion suits, and I can attest that they are very bulky, and it's exhausting to maneuver in them.

If your brand has a head pillow, inflate it. This feature gives an added measure of buoyancy to the head and airway, especially in rough seas. Immersion suits never have gas-charged fill systems for the head pillows. And unlike most vest oral inflation tubes, immersion suit head pillows will have a cap or sheath to push down while inflating. You can use fingers or the front edge of your teeth to depress the mechanism and blow into the tube.

Scuba

Though I have numerous technical and medical diving certifications, I am not qualified to instruct scuba and won't be discussing this discipline in detail. The skills needed to safely scuba dive are an entire book on its own, but there are a few simple tenets of basic dive safety.

Common sense dictates that you never scuba dive without proper training. Otherwise, it's a recipe for disaster. Scuba diving is relatively safe, but it requires many hours in both the classroom and in the water to become just marginally proficient. Get certified by a recognized and respected dive master. Once certified, initially you should dive with more experienced divers. However, don't let anyone of any experience level goad you into unsafe diving or diving beyond your capabilities.

Get certified in the United States. The regulations in foreign countries can be extremely lax, and many of these foreign dive sites are motivated by dollars. Though there are obviously reputable dive centers around the globe, tourist-centric facilities can rush students through the process so that they can get their clients diving and paying. You can't learn to dive in an hour. I know someone who got "certified" at a dive site in the Caribbean. After a half-hour lesson in the pool, he was taken out for a hundred-foot dive! I have been certified for decades, and I've never been that deep. No novice diver should ever be that deep, especially on the very first dive.

Though it is a relatively safe activity, tragedies occur, and they are preventable. The Divers Alert Network (DAN) publishes statistics every year on scuba diving injuries and fatalities. According to their research, some very clear data has emerged; most scuba divers drown with air still in their tanks. The majority were experienced divers, and those who weren't were often with experienced divers who led them into trouble. (Other factors include dehydration, drugs and/or alcohol, and obesity.)[4]

The Fate of the Galaxy

Captain Dave Shoemaker spent more than twenty-five years working the waters of the Bering Sea and thought he had seen all of its conditions. But this tale demonstrates how quickly things can go wrong on the water and how deadly the outcome can be, even for the most experienced seaman.

On October 20, 2002, Shoemaker and his crew were hard at work aboard the 180-foot fish processor *Galaxy*. They were positioned in the Bering Sea some thirty miles southwest of Saint Paul Island. For most mariners, the conditions would have been horrendous—fifty-plus-knot winds and waves in excess of twenty feet. But for Shoemaker, who spent more than a quarter century plying the frigid waters off Alaska, the day was routine.

"The day was typical for us … no different than any other commute," Shoemaker recalled in an interview I conducted in 2014.

However, as the seas began to build late in the afternoon, the ship was hit by a large wave on the starboard stern quarter. At the time, Shoemaker was in the galley, grabbing a quick bite to eat. Though Shoemaker felt the wave and thought it had struck the vessel hard, he was engrossed in getting back to his responsibilities and did not believe the situation merited inspection. Minutes later, smoke began to engulf all levels of the vessel, including the bridge. Initial firefighting actions by the crew unfortunately created a back-draft explosion, sending three men into the forty-degree water. Fire, man-overboard, and abandonment emergencies occurred all at the same moment.

"I said, 'This cannot be happening,'" Shoemaker recalled.

In a very short time, the ship was without power, as all systems were compromised by the fire. Most of the safety equipment was destroyed as well, including rafts and many of the immersion suits. Emergency action plans were rendered useless as the complexity of the crisis began to overwhelm the crew.

"We had to respond defensively rather than offensively. When Jerry Stevens (one of the men thrown into the water by the back-draft explosion) died in view of all the crew, the intensity escalated five hundredfold. With smoke, an explosion, three men in the water, and loss of life all within the first five minutes, it brought reality straight to the gut," Shoemaker said.

Decisions were made in an attempt to adapt to the crisis. Man-overboard rescues were performed as the ship was being abandoned. Shoemaker had to evacuate the ship from the roof of the bridge wheelhouse, where the survivors had retreated from the fire.

"I'm asking people to jump off the back of a boat that's thirty-four feet out of the water at the dock, and add twenty foot seas to that. You've got forty, forty-five, fifty feet, and these kids are standing back there, petrified," Shoemaker recounted. "Not only am I going to have them jump off the back of the boat, I'm going to have them jump out of a four-story building."

The compounding of the emergency was staggering, according to Shoemaker. Crew members valiantly risked their lives to pull the men from the water. Shoemaker desperately tried to find a way to send a distress message as the vessel burned around him. The flames became so intense that at one point Shoemaker realized the heat had melted the radio mic cord in his hand. Safety equipment was destroyed, and the vessel was dead in the water in horrendous and deteriorating conditions.

"This was a two-and-a-half-hour deal while no one knew what we were dealing with. No one knows!" Shoemaker recalled.

In a truly remarkable occurrence, with a handheld radio Shoemaker was able to reach an employee who was monitoring a LORAN (long range navigation) station on Saint Paul Island, nearly thirty-five miles away. A transmission at that distance by handheld radio is unheard of, and this particular station hadn't been manned in five years. The person was scheduled to be picked up that day when the distress call came in. The SOS call was relayed from there to the Coast Guard and other vessels in the area.

Shoemaker and his crew were able to save twenty-three of the twenty-six people on board, but Shoemaker is still haunted by the three lives lost. He has made it his mission to relate his experience to anyone who might face an emergency on the water in the hope that it will prevent another disaster like the *Galaxy*'s. Several of the crew, including Shoemaker, received medals from the Coast Guard for their courage that day. There are true tales of selflessness from that day. One NOAA observer who was on board gave up her immersion suit to an injured survivor and entered the water in only her pajamas. She miraculously survived more than an hour and a half in the water.

Shoemaker, however, cares little for accolades. His priority now is to educate other mariners.

"I spend all my time training others since the accident. After leaving the hospital in 2003 [Shoemaker suffered a number of serious injuries, including extensive burns and broken ribs], I opted to become the safety director to the very company that employed me as a captain of the *Galaxy*. I spent approximately five years writing a safety manual and became a certified instructor for NPFVOA [North Pacific Vessels Owners Association]. Since then I have been in front of USCG, NOAA, [and] private civilian organizations, both in the USA and Canada," Shoemaker said.

I have had the honor of attending a lecture by Captain Shoemaker at the US Coast Academy in New London, Connecticut, when he spoke to a class of NOAA (National Oceanic and Atmospheric Administration) recruits and staff, as he does every year. All who attended were reminded of how little any of us knows when Mother Nature takes the reins.

Shoemaker emphasized this point.

"More time spent on the water without incident can be extremely damaging to acceptance that something could happen. Having spent twenty-five years on the water, what took place on

October 20, 2002, was the farthest thing from my mind. I see this time and time again with commercial participants in my drill classes. They just do not think that anything like this would ever happen to them. Therefore, officers do not pass the possibilities on to the crew or passengers."

Captain Shoemaker takes full responsibility for the *Galaxy* disaster. Despite the fact that his actions undoubtedly saved lives that day, he is open about what he perceives as his failures during the incident.

When asked what he would have done differently, Shoemaker paused then said, "There are countless 'single most important things' that I did not do. To isolate the one that is most important is difficult. I would say that considering the possibility that something like this could have ever happen to me would be a key. However, not responding the very second that I was informed that there was smoke in the factory was huge. That said, what if I was not able to have made a radio call after the battle started? I spent too much time qualifying the smoke instead of immediately radioing our problem and not in responding to a life-threatening issue."

An important aspect of the crisis that Shoemaker emphasizes is how quickly it overwhelmed the vessel and the crew. Despite his experience and training, nothing could have prepared him for the emergency that was unfolding. According to Shoemaker, no matter how long you have been on the water, every day is your first day. No matter how many waves, storms, or dangers you have faced, Mother Nature always bats last. Shoemaker had been a captain in some of the most dangerous waters on the planet and thought he had experienced and dealt with all that the ocean could throw his way.

His most important recommendation is to never become complacent on the water.

"I would have been more proactive in drills on board. [Shoemaker and his crew did partake in practice drills and were fully compliant with all USCG regulations.] I would have made sure that every person on board knew ten times more [than he did] about every safety device on board. Drills would have been conducted more extensively; thinking outside the box would have been shared with everyone. More importantly, I would make sure that every person knew the proper procedure of drill components. And probably the most important issue would have been the proper use of the EPIRB [emergency position indicating radio beacon] and how it actually works," said Shoemaker.

In the confusion, Shoemaker forgot that an electronic locator beacon was located just outside the wheelhouse. Had it been activated, it instantly would have begun alerting the coast guard of the emergency. Compounding the mistake, no one but Shoemaker knew what it was and how it worked.

In the end, one crew member perished as a result of the initial explosion. He was thrown into the water by the force of the back draft and though courageous attempts were made to retrieve him, he did not survive. Another became entangled in lines in an attempt to jump from the bridge and suffocated. The last man, unfortunately, did not make it to the life raft after jumping from the top of the wheelhouse and was swept away. His body was recovered six months later, still in his survival suit.

Lessons Learned

- Shoemaker's main recommendation is not to get complacent. Time on the water can be an enemy to survival if it blinds you to the belief that an emergency can't happen to you. "Never take for granted that your vessel will return to port with you on it!" Shoemaker said.

- Never wrap lines around your body or any body part. At one point Shoemaker almost lost his hand when he was attempting to deploy a life raft while trying to keep it under control by wrapping the line around his hand.

- Life rafts have a lifeline. Though counter to most life raft entry recommendations, Shoemaker had his men jump directly into the raft from the top of the bridge. Though this was dangerous and normally would not be recommended, it was a worst-case scenario, and Shoemaker's decision saved lives. The one man who missed the raft was swept away by the current and perished. If Shoemaker or any of his crew had known about the raft's lifeline, they might have been able to rescue him. (See chapter 6 for information on the location and use of life raft lifelines.)

- Make sure all your crew know where, how, and when to use all safety devices on the vessel. If the captain is the sole repository of emergency information and something happens to him or her, these items will become useless to other survivors.

- If you have to ask yourself the question "Should I check that?" or "I wonder if that's a problem?" it probably is, and you probably should. React at the first sign of a problem. Don't wait until an emergency has gotten out of control to begin dealing with it.

After the Galaxy is among several books on this incident. You can go online and search "tragedy and courage on the Bering Sea" or "F/V Galaxy Capt. Dave Shoemaker" and see selected sections of the DVD. This chapter includes sections from this DVD and from multiple interviews with Captain Shoemaker in 2014.

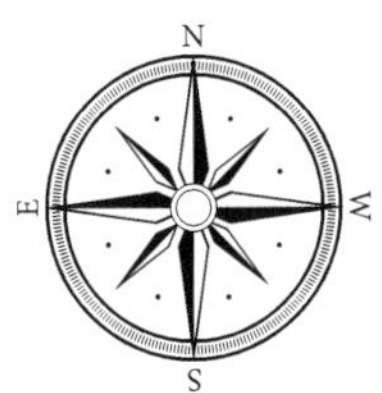

5 Emergency Swimming

How do you decide whether to swim for safety in an emergency?

Several important criteria should be considered before you even enter the water, especially if you don't have swimming experience or if the area is unfamiliar to you. Rip currents get their own special chapter because of how hazardous they are, but never swim in a rip. Don't go out if rips are present, even if you are a strong swimmer. Pay attention to the water. Are other swimmers out? If they are, what are they doing? Are they all up and down the beach or in one spot? Try to read what is happening before you enter. Ask a lifeguard; if you can't find one, ask a local. "Why is everybody swimming in this spot and not a hundred yards away?" The answer you get could save your life.

Never enter swift water.

Swift water may be the most hazardous of all water emergencies. People very rarely survive when they are swept away by moving water. It requires intense training to overcome swift-water emergencies. Rescue and emergency personnel lose their lives in swift water, despite their training. One misstep or fall, and a life will be lost. Don't let it be yours.

When to Swim for It

If you find yourself in an emergency and at the mercy of the water, you can apply practical skills to increase your odds of survival.

So, when do you swim for it? When is it too far?

The decision can be a matter of life or death in an emergency, and there are conflicting opinions on the best way to survive. Some experts advocate swimming when possible, and some are proponents of going with the flow. Based on my training and years of water experience, swim only short distances for very specific reasons, and simply go with the flow.

There are epic case histories of swims for survival, several of which will be described later in this chapter, but they are very rare. Some of the toughest and most experienced watermen have died trying to outswim Mother Nature. Don't fight her.

So what, exactly, do you do?

There are a number of variables in the decision to swim. Are you injured? When did you last eat? (You'll need those calories.) Do you have a reasonable chance of being rescued? How cold is the water?

The decision to swim is important and not an easy one. When you move, you are making a trade-off. Your movements may be of benefit, but it will cost you energy, energy that you will need to help fend off hypothermia and continue swimming.

Those of us in the survival industry at one time used specific criteria for making the decision to swim. From the water, if you cannot discern shingles on the roof of a building or individual leaves on a tree, you are probably too far out to swim. But what if it's night, or there are no buildings to view, or it's autumn, or there are no trees? With your head only inches above the surface, it may be impossible to determine exactly how far you are from safety. Accurate water-distance judging is a notoriously fickle skill. Many a seafarer has lost his or her life based on misperceptions of distance on the water.

This theory has been reevaluated, and it is now the recommendation that victims swim only short distances for very specific reasons: to get to something good (life raft, shore, another survivor) or to get away from something bad (debris, fire, caustic fluids).[1]

If you are unsure of where you are or where land or rescue might be, adopt the HELP position or simply float on your back.

Don't swim for the sake of swimming.

Have a specific goal in mind if you decide to move. Your survival instinct may be telling you to do something, but in many cases staying put is the best alternative. It doesn't make any sense, if you are six miles from shore, to spend energy and time swimming five of those miles and still be a mile from safety. Conserve energy and calories, and adopt a hypothermia mitigation posture. Every movement will use energy and accelerate the onset of hypothermia.

Keep in mind that in most emergencies, rescuers will be looking for you close to the sinking, ditch site, or reported overboard position. Your swimming may make it harder for rescuers to locate you.

HELP #2
Photo: Ben Rayner

Above is the HELP position (heat escape lessening posture). This is the recommended hypothermia mitigation technique if you go into the water by yourself. It can be enhanced with the use of a contractor's-grade trash bag. Keep one in your vest or survival kit.

Moving as a Group

If you are with other survivors, always swim together toward the target. In many case histories where one individual was tasked with trying to swim for help or a life raft, that person either perished or was the only survivor.

Make the group's goal as short and specific as possible.

As with single-swimmer recommendations, swim only to get away from bad or to get to something good.

The best method for group movement is called the chain formation. With all survivors oriented one behind the other and facing the same direction while floating on your backs, hook your legs around the person in front of you. Your feet should go underneath the armpits of the person who is two people in the chain in front of you. The person at the head of the chain is the captain and should shout out a cadence with as few syllables as possible, such as "arms up; stroke" or simply "arms; stroke." This will keep everyone together—and this is critical. This formation works most effectively when conducted in unison. It becomes less so when survivors are unsynchronized.

The captain or the person shouting cadence needs to be loud and must do this over water and waves splashing in his or her face, so make sure the captain is comfortable with that task. Be aware that it is not a race. Go steady and slowly. (During training I often observed students unnecessarily speed through the chain formation drill. This will exhaust even experienced swimmers very quickly.) Try to perform this movement with everyone together, pulling as a single stroke. It will be far more efficient than with a haphazard series of strokes.

The last person at the end of the chain should not stroke. This person should keep his or her hands clasped around the feet of the person behind him or her and lightly flutter-kick so as to lessen drag on the formation. Use very slow and steady kicking. If you kick furiously, you will tire very quickly and become a drag on the rest of the chain. If you are in an immersion suit, just float; don't kick at all. These suits float the wearer high in the water, and the buoyancy of the suit will prevent you from kicking anyway.

If the person in front of you begins to pull away or the formation breaks down, grab him or her by the vest or shoulders, and pull the formation back together. Don't hesitate to stop the formation and regroup if is not making progress or is falling apart.

The benefits of this formation are that you keep all survivors together while still sharing body heat. However, this formation will still be an energy drain, as the large muscle groups are not used. Also, keeping survivors together is vital in maintaining the morale of the group. The loss of fellow survivors during an emergency has proven to compound the psychological stresses of survival. Mental energy spent on wondering or worrying about where other survivors are can cause victims to succumb. Try to keep the group together at all times.

For long distances, this formation or any swimming is not recommended.

Chain Formation

Photo: Ben Rayner

The chain formation. The more coordinated the stroking action is, the more efficient this technique will be. Also, once there are more than seven to eight people, break the chain into two separate groups. The more people in the chain, the more difficult it is to coordinate and execute. Make sure your feet are securely hugging the person in front of you.

Emergency Swimming

There are specific scenarios where attempting a swim could increase your chances of survival. Remember, however, that a majority of emergencies will demand that you not swim for it.

Based on data and my experience in the water, I instruct all my students to go with the flow. Humans simply are not efficient in the water. Even a strong and experienced swimmer can only manage one mile per hour or so. And that is for a limited period. If you are trying to counter an opposing current of only half a knot, all of your energy will be wasted—energy that you will need to survive. If forces are pushing you (wind, waves, tides, or currents), even if it is away from land or safety, go along for the ride. Your chances of survival decrease if you fight against prevailing forces.

Case histories can be found of people making epic swims, even in cold water, but they are truly the exception rather than the rule. For every one case of a victim's attempting and making a long swim, there are dozens, if not hundreds, every year in the United States where people have perished after making an ill-fated decision to swim for it.[2]

The classic example is of lifeguard and all-around waterman Eddie Aikau. Despite being credited with inventing modern lifeguarding and saving more lives in the water than any other human, Aikau lost his own when he made an ill-fated decision to swim for help after a boat capsized off the coast of Lanai in March 1978. According to the other survivors, Aikau also removed his life vest before attempting to paddle a surfboard twelve miles in heavy seas back to land, countering one of the basic elements of safety at sea. Neither his board nor his body were ever recovered.[3]

One note on removal of clothes and shoes: the industry recommendation is to keep everything on. The insulating properties will be beneficial, and contrary to common sense, boots will not drag you to the bottom. Footwear is most often positively buoyant, and unless it becomes an obvious impediment it should be kept on. An exception would be waders, especially in high-sea states or strong currents.

Having been knocked, ripped, and otherwise abused by wind, waves, and currents in several oceans and most of the Great Lakes, my advice is to go with the flow. I have been just feet from shore in conditions where not even Olympian Michael Phelps could have countered the forces of nature and reached safety. I also have been in conditions where a mile of water was covered in a matter of minutes by swimming with and not against the prevailing conditions.

Though the psychological strain that develops when you are being pulled from the safety of shore can be overwhelming, it is better to be dragged away from safety than to perish trying to reach it. This is the reason why many people, even those with swimming experience, drown in rip currents. When victims realize they are being pulled out to sea, the natural reaction is to swim like mad, expending all of their energy, both physical and mental.

Whether in a shore rip or ocean current, just go with the conditions. If they are bringing you where you want to go, that is a plus; if they are dragging you away from land or safety, that isn't good, but it isn't necessarily a fatal situation either.

Also remember to swim on your back if you have a flotation device. Natural swimming styles with a donned vest will be very difficult to manage, as they create drag and burn far more energy. Simply lie on your back, and use back strokes. You will still make progress, but you also will conserve the calories that you will need to keep you alive.

The following story reveals how quickly even a seasoned waterman can get into a deadly situation.

Man Overboard

The first sharks showed up less than an hour after John Aldridge fell off his boat in July 2013. He was forty miles off Montauk, New York, and the man-overboard call wouldn't be made for another three hours. His tale of how he survived more than twelve hours in seventy-two-degree water in the open Atlantic is truly remarkable. Though his experience is the exception rather than the rule, his ability to focus and improvise saved his life and has valuable lessons for all mariners.

At approximately three thirty in the morning on July 24, 2013, Aldridge and his business partner and good friend Anthony Sosinski, along with another friend hired for the trip, Mike Migliaccio, were under way toward the forty-fathom curve, a favored fishing ground, to pull and set their traps from their vessel, the forty-five-foot *Anna Mary*. Aldridge and Sosinski had bought the lobster boat in 2006 and had forged a living setting more than eight hundred traps. Twice a week the partners would take overnight trips to pull and reset their gear.

On the evening of the incident, anxious to work, Aldridge piloted the boat and set the deck, while Sosinski and Migliaccio caught a few precious hours of sleep before an eighteen-hour-work day. While moving a two-hundred-pound ice cooler across the deck, the handle snapped, sending Aldridge reeling backward and off the open-transom vessel.

That was just the beginning of his nightmare.

As the vessel pulled away under autopilot in the darkness at six and a half knots, the reality of his situation was all too evident, according to Aldridge. His shouts for help went unheard to his crew below deck. Alone, at night, in very chilling water, Aldridge said he quickly realized that he would need to get his panic under control and focus if he was going to survive the ordeal.

"It seemed like from the time the handle actually broke until I went off the back of the boat, so much went through my head. It might have only been a tenth of a second, but so many things went through my mind," said Aldridge. "By the time I hit the water I was in disbelief. I thought to myself, 'I just can't believe this is happening to me.' No one was aware, the boat was pulling away, and I panicked. I thought I had just made the biggest mistake of my life, and it was going to kill me."

One of his first clear thoughts was that his boots would make an excellent flotation device. Though waders and some footwear can cause a person to sink, most footwear floats and can actually be useful in water emergencies. On the docks, fellow fishermen in the past had ribbed him about his choice of footwear. Aldridge quickly ascertained that he could use his boots as an improvised life preserver and minimize energy loss.

"At first I was kind of flailing, and I couldn't get my feet under me. That's when I realized my boots are buoyant. I kicked my boots off and grabbed hold of them," Aldridge recalled. "I was able to catch my breath and relax at that point and start to think and analyze the situation."

Aldridge turned the boots upside down to trap air inside them and tucked them under his armpits, making a very effective flotation system that helped save his life.

Throughout the ordeal, sharks were a constant threat, and he was dive-bombed by sea birds, bitten by sea lice, and even a pesky sunfish paid a visit, but nothing could shake his spirit.

"At one point I was like, 'C'mon! I am trying to survive here,'" Aldridge recalled with a laugh.

Though physically affected by the cold and waves, his ability to stay positive was a huge factor in his survival, according to Aldridge. Without prior training, he was able to carefully balance the reality of his predicament and the positive mental focus needed to sustain a calm psychological state.

"I really went into survival mode quite quickly, but some calmness came over me as well," Aldridge recalled. "I had a sense of 'I can get through this.' It was completely a mental game. Of course it was physical, but it was mostly mental."

According to many survival experts, a realistic appraisal of the situation is beneficial in these types of survival emergencies. "Anything negative I tried to push away, but I also still had to deal with it. Staying positive was everything. It meant everything to me. Thinking positive is what saved my life. I simply said, '[F—] you! I ain't gonna die.'"

The coast guard, along with numerous other vessels on the water, including many fellow fishermen, began searching an area estimated to be the size of Rhode Island. Unable to correctly estimate when Aldridge went into the water and how currents would have affected the search area, the USCG initially began their search thirty miles from where he actually was.

"I could hear the helicopters when daylight came, but they missed me. I could tell they were moving away. That was bad and good," Aldridge said. "They weren't finding me, but at least I knew they were looking for me, and I held on to the thought that they were looking for me and they would find me."

Aldridge's ability to keep his panic under control saved his life. Though his visibility was impaired by the wave height, at the top of each wave Aldridge scanned the water for anything that might increase his chances of survival. When daylight came, he spied lobster trawl buoys in the distance. After initially making no headway in trying to swim for the buoy, Aldridge had the presence of mind to realize there would be another buoy down current in the other direction. Rather than exhausting himself in a futile effort, he switched course and calmly rode the current to the next buoy down the line.

When Aldridge realized searchers were pulling away from his position (at one point he actually spied the *Anna Mary* and Sosinski searching for him a quarter mile away) and not expecting him to be in a fixed position on a buoy, he cut the line, used the buoy for flotation, and began moving east with the current and into the search area.

With help from Sosinski on board the *Anna Mary*, other mariners, and the coast guard, Aldridge was finally spotted and picked up after almost fourteen hours in the water.

When asked if he now wears a life vest, Aldridge jokes, "Yeah, I got my boots on all the time."

Humor aside, Aldridge said that during winter work he always has a vest on and that all crew members now have electronic locator beacons on them at all times while onboard the vessel.

The experience hasn't changed his love for the water or his passion for his profession.

"Occasionally, a wave will remind me of what happened, but I don't really think about it. I think it affected my friends and family more than it did me," said Aldridge. "I go to work, I go out, and I come back."

This section is from an interview with survivor John Aldridge conducted by the author over the course of several sessions in February 2015. Read John's entire saga in his recently published work, A Speck in the Sea: A Story of Survival and Rescue, by John Aldridge and Anthony Sosinski.

Swift-Water Emergencies

Of all the aquatic dangers people can face, swift water may be the most hazardous. I lost a relative to a swift-water tragedy, and the consequences are devastating to families. Stay away from swift water at all costs, whether you know how to swim or not.

I have had some limited training in swift water, but I am not a qualified swift-water specialist. However, I can relate what all swift-water specialists recommend: absolutely stay away from swift water, especially children.

Swift-water fatalities happen just that way—swiftly. Don't be lulled into a sense of safety by wearing a life vest near running water. A vest should be worn at all times, but in swift water a vest can also present hazards as well as protect you from them. According to the National Weather Service, just a foot of moving water can move a car; think about what that can do to a human.

The only informed advice I can provide, other than to stay away from moving water, is to adopt the HELP position immediately if you fall into moving water with a vest on. If you are not wearing a vest, try to float on your back to minimize snag hazards. One danger of swift water is having your legs caught by objects under the surface. The rushing liquid force can pin victims underwater, sometimes with their airways just inches below the surface.

Rip Currents

What is a rip current?

Rips are properly called currents, not tides. They form as a result of wave action on the sand and are a common factor in drownings that occur on ocean beaches. You can learn how to avoid them and get out of them with just a few simple facts.

Rip currents occur when wave and wind action deposit sand, building up ridges or sandbars that run roughly parallel to the beach. These sandbars morph and shift throughout the course of a day. They are affected by the tide, the size of the waves, and the direction of the swell. Water collects behind these sandbars as wave-driven water washes up onto the beach, and when a section of the bar gives way, this water rushes through the break and back out to sea perpendicular to the coastline, creating a rip current.

Often you can observe this phenomenon from the beach. Sandy or brown-colored water often can be seen from shore as it heads out to sea. Keep this in mind if you are going in the water.

According to oceanographers, these currents can extend from 200 to 2,500 feet from shore, but they typically are less than thirty feet wide. Rip currents can move at more than five miles per hour.

Even experienced swimmers can only manage one mile per hour, which means there is no chance of outswimming a rip.[4]

Many people have a misconception about rip currents, especially in light of the now-defunct term "rip tides." These currents are just that: currents that travel from the beach and head back out to sea. However, they have finite power and will not carry you so far out that a swim back is not possible. Most rips travel only a short distance from the beach, and as the water behind the bar drains, they slowly ebb and stop. In large surf, rips can carry a person a hundred yards or more out to sea, but most are of fairly short distance and duration and may only carry you a few yards. However, if you get pulled out over your head and can no longer stand, it really doesn't matter how far you traveled to get there. The good news is that all rips eventually stall out and ebb. The latest research seems to show that rips actually flow back to shore eventually in many circumstances.

Rips also can form along jetties and piers, where they can be especially hazardous. During the writing of this book I was caught in a rip on the beach where I learned to surf, forcing me into the rocks. Without the quick action of a fellow surfer, I am not sure I would have been able to extricate myself from the water. I knew there were rips present, and I simply did not analyze the situation thoroughly enough before entering the water. One leg cramp later and I found myself, the water-safety expert, in real trouble. This incident is proof that even experienced water folks can get into danger, and quickly. Take the time to read the water!

Contrary to some beliefs about rips, they do not pull you underwater or drag you down. If you are standing in a rip, it is certainly possible to be knocked off your feet, but you won't be forced underwater. The reason people die is because they panic and furiously begin trying to swim against the current, which saps their strength. Being carried out to sea and away from land will panic even an experienced swimmer, but not even an Olympic medalist can fight against the most modest rip current.

To get a feel of a rip and the power they generate, stand in knee-deep water on a beach with just mild waves. You should be able to feel quite a strong counter force as the water rushes back out to sea between waves. Most folks call that the undertow, and anyone who grew up around waves was lectured by Mom on its power. The undertow technically isn't a rip current, but a rip current is essentially a focused undertow. Imagine that power magnified into a constricted funnel of a rip.

Rip Current

Photo: Nick Steers

In the above picture, the arrow points to the rip as it flows away from the beach. The current can easily be identified by the brown, sandy water. Also note the swirling water at its terminus, called the head. This part of the rip can continue to confuse swimmers and pose a danger. Calmly swim to either side of a rip, and you will eventually be able to freely swim back to the beach.

How can you avoid rip currents?

Avoiding currents is easiest by simply staying out of the water, especially if you are not a strong swimmer. If you do enter the water, only swim at beaches where lifeguards are present. If you are in doubt about whether rip currents are forming, then don't go in the water. Keep in mind that even experienced swimmers drown as a result of rip currents. More than one hundred deaths a year are attributed to rips in the United States. According to the National Weather Service, 80 percent of beach rescues by lifeguards involve rip currents.[5] (A 2013 study from Australia estimated that rip currents are responsible for more deaths annually than floods, cyclones, sharks, and bush fires combined.)[6]

However, should you find yourself being dragged out to sea by a rip, you must do what at first seems the least likely action: enjoy the ride.

No one can fight the power of even a minor rip, so relax and enjoy the ride. Eventually, you will begin to feel the rip easing. When you do, swim parallel to the beach to get out of the rip and then angle back to shore. You don't necessarily need to wait until you've come to a complete stop to begin the task of getting to safety. You can begin to swim parallel to shore to escape the rip's funnel, but take it slowly and methodically. Get your breathing under control, while trying not to struggle or panic.

Keep in mind that as the rip ebbs, a large mass of swirling water, called the head or terminus, can form. (See picture above.) This water may be swirling in multiple directions, so calmly try to move one way or the other to escape the water action. The bigger the surf, the bigger and stronger the rip currents, so stay calm and simply move parallel to the beach until you can swim directly in. This is easier said than done, especially for a struggling swimmer.

Another peril in rips caused by larger surf is getting caught in the impact zone of the waves.

This is the last place any struggling swimmer wants to be. The impact zone is where the waves are crashing. If caught in this area, the waves break directly onto any swimmers, which forces them under and holds them down. The only solution is to continue to head farther out to pass by the impact zone. Anyone caught in the impact zone is in immediate danger and needs to get out as quickly as possible or be rescued.

Stay away from structures, especially in high-surf conditions or where currents of any kind are present.

IF CAUGHT IN A RIP CURRENT

- Don't fight the current
- Swim out of the current, then to shore
- If you can't escape, float or tread water
- If you need help, call or wave for assistance

SAFETY

- Know how to swim
- Never swim alone
- If in doubt, don't go out

More information about rip currents can be found at the following web sites:

www.ripcurrents.noaa.gov
www.usla.org

Break the Grip of the Rip

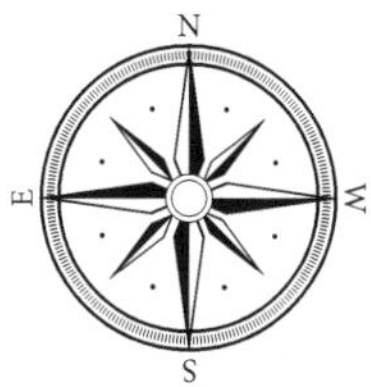

6

Boating Safety and Emergency Equipment

Anyone who owns a boat should be properly licensed and take a boating-specific water-safety course. However, whenever on a boat or dock or otherwise on the water, individuals, no matter what age, should be in properly fitting life vests. If you are on a vessel, life vests should be worn at all times, especially on children. If you are on a vessel of any size that does not have properly fitting vests for all individuals, do not board. If you are invited out for a day of fun on the water with a neighbor or relative, and vests are not available for you or your children, do not board the vessel.

According to the USCG, many marine drownings occur at the dock. Do not be lulled into a sense of security because the vessel you are on is ensconced in a slip. Accidental and intentional fall/dive accidents account for many water-related deaths. Though marinas have begun to heed the call for safety ladders and accessible egress points for their docks, many still have not implemented these designs. In cold-water situations, lack of escape points and ladders at marinas have been cited as contributing causes in drownings. No matter your fitness level, you may not be able to pull yourself back up onto a dock after falling in the water, especially in cold water. Wear a life vest at all times when you and your family are on the water—this includes at the dock.

If you do find yourself in open water and in trouble, the following techniques have been proven to save lives.

The Survival Pattern

When it comes to boating safety, preventing emergencies must be paramount for any captain and for any passenger aboard a vessel. Whether you find yourself in the open ocean like John Aldridge or have fallen off the dock, the survival pattern can help you stay alive.

Whether you are ten feet or ten miles from shore, you should wear a life vest at all times. No exceptions. Enhance your life vest with some basic safety items—an electronic locator beacon, if available; a whistle or noise maker; a flashlight or some sort of illumination; and a trash bag for enhancement of the HELP position.

Regardless of whether your emergency is five minutes or five days and whether you are in a life raft or in the water, there is a technique to keep you alive called the *survival pattern*. Before we implement these skills, I will stress again that it is imperative to know and understand all of your safety and survival gear before you find yourself at the mercy of a gale in fifty-degree water. Taking the time to understand your life raft and its contents with your crew at the start of the season may be the most practical way for mariners to survive a sea emergency.

The survival pattern has four phases:

- protection
- first aid

- signaling devices
- endurance

For more than thirty years this method has proven to extend survival times. The survival pattern allows for a more comprehensive understanding of why and how people survive water-related emergencies.

Protection

This first phase of the survival pattern is called protection and it is just that: protect yourself from the elements.

If you are in the water, adopt the HELP position or carpet formation, and save energy.

If you are inside your raft, pull Velcro, lines, and lanyards, and engage zippers to protect occupants from the elements. Life raft Velcro is usually of an industrial grade and will often need to be manipulated with both hands; it won't separate with a one-handed tug. In the Northeast, protection usually will mean shielding from the cold, even in the summer months. In a tropical environment, that may mean opening up ports or vents, or even removing the canopy altogether. If you remove a canopy for thermal regulation, it will expose you directly to the power of the sun. Make sure to protect skin with sunscreen, which usually comes in most life raft kits. You can also repurpose a bag, fabric or plastic, from the raft kit as a sun barrier.

This phase also includes removing all water from the raft.

Utilize the raft's collapsible bailing bucket to remove all water. Keep in mind that water pulls heat and energy away from the body twenty-four to twenty-five times faster than air, so every last drop, even the sheen on the bottom of the raft, needs to be removed.[1] Use one of the raft sponges to wipe up all of the water to make the raft as dry as possible.

The next step is to get seasickness tablets into survivors as soon as possible. Seasickness is no joke. It can kill you by simple dehydration and, even more insidiously, by sapping your will to live. Even if you consider your stomach iron-cast and immune to this malady, in the confines of a raft, compounded by injury or especially the smell of others vomiting, you'll be as susceptible to motion sickness as the greenest landlubber. There are numerous case histories of marine survivors giving up and perishing simply because of seasickness. Survivors have related that they became so overwhelmed by seasickness that their will to live became a wish to die. (See the end of this chapter for a full explanation of seasickness.)

It is also recommended to set up a watch as soon as possible. In the first hours, assign survivors short duration periods. Set up a watch even in the carpet formation. Some members can fall asleep or rest while others remain on watch.

If the conditions are rough, utilize the foul-weather port of the raft. This is standard on most rafts and is located in the canopy ceiling. It allows survivors to stick a head out to observe conditions, while keeping the raft and its occupants dry. Keep these shifts short. The watch person will have to squat, making long stretches of observation very uncomfortable. For the first few hours, shift people every twenty minutes or so to avoid fatigue. The foul-weather port also can be utilized for rainwater collection by tying it off from the inside.

Finally, choose someone who is clear-headed and preferably uninjured to gather up all the signaling devices and place them in one of the stowage pockets that ring the inside of the raft.

First Aid

Once inside the raft, assess the condition of survivors. Frankly, if there are severe internal or head injuries, there is little treatment for these serious conditions—even by someone with advanced medical training—inside a life raft with an unstable bottom. Keep victims warm to help stave off shock and hypothermia. For severe wounds, apply direct pressure to stop any bleeding. (Even severe lacerations can be mitigated with direct pressure.) Place any broken limbs in a position of comfort.

Adrenaline can mask very serious wounds. As it begins to wear off, a survivor's condition can deteriorate rapidly. After the first half hour or so, reassess survivors and observe their current status. When it comes to first aid, the psychological treatment will be the most beneficial. (More about this topic in the endurance phase.)

Also, CPR is much less effective and more difficult to perform with the spongy, unstable materials of a raft. Compressions are the most important aspect of CPR, and they are much less effective when the patient is not on a hard, stable surface. In a pinch, if there is a healthy survivor, have him or her lie facedown on the raft bottom, place the victim on top of this person, face up, and perform CPR. This is not ideal, but it may provide enough stability to make the technique effective.

Signaling Devices

As part of the protection phase, gather up all signaling devices. If you are in the water without a raft and have devices, make sure you can access them. Know where they are and how they work. Will you be able to manipulate and activate the devices with cold fingers?

If you are in a raft, consolidate the items and place them in a stowage pocket near the main boarding entrance of the raft. Assign a survivor, preferably someone uninjured and clear-headed, to take stock of the signaling devices. Read directions while you have available light. Make sure that someone understands their proper use. In theory, they are easy to use; in the throes of an emergency, it can be far more complicated. Do not wait until you hear the sound of a rescue craft to start trying to find the devices or utilize them. Survivors have sunk their rafts in the excitement of trying to signal rescuers.

Usually a kit will include daytime and nighttime devices. Day devices include a signaling mirror (or heliograph). Coast guard personnel cite mirrors or even improvised reflective devices as the best way, short of EPIRBs, to attract rescuers in an emergency.

There are drawings on the back of the mirrors to explain their function. But the use of signal mirrors is a great opportunity for preplanning. Five minutes of training while at the dock can save lives. Heliographs also can be used at night if there is strong moonlight.

Rescue streamers are another important item to have on your raft. If your raft doesn't have them, they can be purchased relatively cheaply for a way to add an extra measure of safety. They are simple, foot-wide, twenty-five- to hundred-foot-long strips of bright plastic that will make you more visible to rescuers. There are also personal streamers that can be attached to a life vest if you are not in a raft.

Sea dyes are usually not part of civilian life-raft emergency kits, but they are also an effective way to become a bigger target. Even in heavy sea states, dyes will remain visible, making a large target for rescuers to follow. Dyes are a great addition to a life vest. Outside of an electronic beacon, dyes can be very effective, whether in the water or in a raft.

Pyrotechnic devices also should be included in your raft or as part of your life vest or safety kit. There are several different styles. Make sure you and your crew know how all of the various styles and brands function. Inspect these devices before the start of every season to ensure they are within the expiration date and are not corroded. Styles include handheld smoke-only flares, can-style smoke flares, handheld flares, and rocket flares.

Smoke and handheld flares are often activated by removing a cap and striking the flare across the surface of the cap. Other brands require the removal of a cap, which allows a small lanyard to drop down. Pulling on the lanyard activates the device. Make sure you manipulate these devices over the side of the raft and away from your face. Heat and flame do not mix with rubber and neoprene. There are case histories of survivors sinking their rafts with misuse of pyrotechnic devices during the stress and anticipation of rescue.

In my experience, almost every brand of smoke or hand flare will emit hot slag, sparks, or embers. Make sure you do not stare directly at handheld flares. The strong illumination factor can permanently damage your retina. Ensure others in the raft know you are deploying these devices so they can look away and protect themselves.

Can-style smoke flares are about the size of a can of tomatoes. Unscrew the cap and gently invert the can once or twice to mix the chemicals; the smoke will begin emitting. Then toss the can into the water away from the raft. Be careful with this style of device; I have seen chemicals leak from the can and burn people. When inverting the can, do it carefully, and when you toss the can, do not wind up and throw a fastball. If it's leaking it can spray the chemicals all over you and the raft. This can-style device will get hot enough to melt the rubber, so make sure you gently toss it underhand, downwind and down current of the raft.

Rocket flares are also included in many rafts. Make sure you do not discharge these or any pyrotechnic device near your face. Turn away when deploying them. These flares are designed to ascend to one thousand feet and burn out approximately one hundred feet above the surface, but they can malfunction. If you are having a really bad day, the flare could come right back down on your raft while still lit. Use a five- to ten-degree angle (off of ninety) when setting off the flare so if this occurs, it will be less likely to come back onto you and the raft. All rocket flares have a cap to unscrew, and a small string or lanyard will drop down. Pull on the lanyard to activate the flare. There will be some recoil to this style of device so be aware of this.

With pyrotechnic devices you must make an educated guess that the person you are trying to signal is actually looking for you. A commercial airliner at thirty-five thousand feet is not searching for you, and even if it was, the crew would never see these styles of signaling devices. (Steve Callahan, author of *76 Days Adrift*, said he was frustrated at how little illumination rocket flares produced during daylight hours.)

Try to keep the devices dry. This may be easier said than done, but some styles of flares have been demonstrated to generate heat when wet. They will usually come in heavy plastic packing so they should be safe from water, but sometimes this packaging prevents the user from reading directions. If you have to remove the packing to read the directions, make sure you keep the device dry and away from water. I am not aware of instances in which these devices activated when they became wet, but they can generate enough heat to be a hazard to the raft and could possibly malfunction when needed.

The best choices for signaling devices are electronic personal locator beacons. There are many styles, brands, and prices, but all essentially work the same way. When it comes to safety, spending an extra hundred dollars is worth the cost. These beacons let rescuers know of an emergency and—important—exactly where you are. Just like any device, make sure you understand how it is used and where it is. Some will automatically deploy; others must be manually deployed.

Be warned: any accidental activation of a locator device will cost you a fine if the US Coast Guard is deployed. A false alarm takes these rescue assets away from other potential emergencies.

Endurance

It is easy to sit behind a computer and write about endurance. It is a whole other story to actually live through an emergency. However, I have spent the better part of decade training, researching, and writing on this topic, and there is a general consensus on the psychology of survival.

Keeping people on an even keel or neutral may be the best tactic to implement in an emergency. Survivors can succumb to the mental and psychological devastation of a sea stranding or any life-threatening emergency simply because they are overwhelmed by the magnitude of the crisis. Helping to bolster the spirits of survivors and being receptive to encouragement can be a vital component of short- or long-term survival. Homicides and suicides have occurred in these situations. Panicked survivors have been tossed out of rafts when their behavior threatened other survivors. Survivors have taken their own lives in desperation and delirium. Don't let victims sink too deep into despair.

The positive end of the spectrum can also affect survival.

There is a documented phenomenon called the Stockdale Paradox.[2] It is named after Admiral James Stockdale, the highest ranking American POW of the Vietnam War. Anecdotal evidence and scientific research seems to support the contention that optimists are often the first to perish in an emergency. I want to be very specific: this isn't to say that being positive, especially in a crisis, is going to kill you. In fact, a positive outlook is a crucial component to survival, as proven by survivor John Aldridge, but extreme optimism seems to drain psychological reserves in many people.

This was dramatically played out in the sinking of the ferry *Estonia* in the Baltic Sea in 1994, which claimed close to one thousand lives. Paul Barney, one of the few survivors, is an often-quoted source in many safety and survival books. After the sinking, Barney made it into a raft with fifteen others. He relates how a person they labeled “Mr. Positive” was one of the first to perish. Of the sixteen people who made it inside the raft, only Barney and five others survived. The rest succumbed to hypothermia and fatigue before rescue.[3]

Psychologists believe the Stockdale Paradox unfolds when survivors pin their hopes on an arbitrary deadline. When that fails to materialize, they simply have no mental reserves to keep pushing on.

The phenomenon is difficult to quantify and study due to its specific parameters, but data clearly indicate that extremes of the psychological spectrum are not conducive to survival. Most experts recommend “realistic optimism,” combining a blunt appreciation of the predicament with a steadfast belief that you can survive. Try to keep survivors on an even keel—that is, not too despondent and not too optimistic. Be aware of the signs in others and yourself. Act quickly to intervene with others, and be receptive to their efforts when they try to assist you.

Further Recommendations

Many experts recommend that no food or water be consumed in the first twenty-four hours of an emergency at sea. Whatever is consumed will eventually have to be expelled, and people have lost their lives by falling off the raft while addressing the need to urinate or defecate. One exception is food for anyone who is conscious and hypothermic. Getting sugar or glucose into hypothermic survivors will allow them to replenish their reserves and is an excellent treatment for hypothermia. Most raft food will have high glucose content for this reason. Remember, they must be conscious. Never put food or water into the mouth of anyone who is unconscious.

Another exception is for those who are dehydrated. Even if they vomit it back up, get water into people who are dehydrated.

The short-term effects are very debilitating, and prolonged dehydration, even over the period of a few hours, can be fatal.

Any movement in the raft will destabilize it, causing frustration with anyone trying to sleep and discomfort for anyone who is injured. The less movement, the better off occupants will be.

Survival relies on comfort. This is a fairly simple idea but one that experts come back to when explaining survivor psychology. The more comfortable you are, the better your odds of survival become. Get your raft dry. Get seasickness tablets into survivors. Understand the use of all signaling devices. Keep survivors realistically hopeful. Do not get overly depressed by your circumstances, and refrain from wide swings of emotion, if possible. Pulling people up and bringing them down psychologically has been proven to extend survival times in real-world emergencies.

Seventy-Six Days Adrift

The history of sea survival counts a number of epic ordeals: the 2013 case of Mexican fisherman Jose Alvarenga, which at first seemed unbelievable but has now been verified, who spent more than thirteen months adrift in the Pacific; Bill and Simonne Butler, a couple who spent sixty-six days lost at sea in 1989; Maurice and Maralyn Bailey, who spent 117 days lost at sea in 1973. However, one of the more dramatic tales of survival is of Steven Callahan, who spent seventy-six days adrift alone in the Atlantic in a life raft before landing ashore in the Caribbean.

Callahan wrote the *New York Times* best-selling book *Adrift: 76 Days Lost at Sea* about his survival, and it has fascinated readers ever since its publication in 1986.

According to Callahan, in February 1981, while navigating his 6.5-meter sloop, the *Napoleon Solo,* several days out from the Azores, he ran into a gale. His boat struck an unknown object during the storm and rapidly began taking on water. The custom-built craft had water-tight compartments, which allowed the mariner precious time to load his life raft with as much gear as possible and to also take a small rubber inflatable boat that proved invaluable during his ordeal. Through sheer ingenuity and determination, Callahan kept himself alive for seventy-six days until he was rescued just offshore of the Caribbean island of Marie Galante by local fishermen.

Though Callahan doesn't measure or compare his survival by the duration, his attitude during his ordeal encapsulates many of the survival techniques now used to train mariners. As a survivor, Callahan is often asked what allowed him to endure and last until rescue. Callahan cited several factors; chief among them was that he had read accounts of other survivors. Callahan noted the overall mind-set of survivors and how they dealt with and reacted to their problems was invaluable.

"I had read survival books as part of my preparation before I went to sea. I got a bit of vicarious information from them. It wasn't that I got an exact tutorial, but just reading about their attitude and approach was helpful. Just getting some perspective that was outside my own experience was the benefit. The details (of their tales) were not as important as the general pattern and their mind-set. I am not a remarkable guy. That is important for everyone to realize. I thought I was done for, but from my reading I knew that these people survived, and if they could do it, I could too. Survival is just like life; it has its ups and downs. It's just that ups and downs are much more extreme," Callahan recalled in an interview with me.

Callahan faced many challenges during his time at sea, but his ability to procure water was the most critical factor of his survival. He had access to several solar stills that eventually allowed him to make his own water, but they were notoriously fickle. According to Callahan, he might be the only long-term survivor to have gotten that style of solar still to work.

Callahan is a frequent speaker and has done extensive research in the field of sea survival. He cannot find a single instance of another survivor getting the still to function and provide water. (Callahan and other marine survivors recommend outfitting yourself with a top-of-the-line desalinator if you navigate offshore.)

When asked what the worst moment was during his ordeal, Callahan has a hard time rating the many perils he faced.

"Just like pain has many forms—throbbing pain, sharp pain, dull pain—survival has several forms. Certainly the boat getting holed and the rush to gather all of the equipment and abandoning the vessel was scary, but once that happened there was a period of recoil from the disaster. I was a survival virgin at that point and didn't really know how to react. I was still trying to figure it all out."

The psychological detriments were real and heavy, according to Callahan.

"Your past failures can come back to haunt you. I thought about all of my mistakes and how I had wished I had done things differently. But as bad as things are you have got to come to grips with it. The quicker you realize 'what is,' the quicker you can deal with it."

Callahan warned of becoming overwhelmed by the reality of an emergency and advised to focus instead on making a balanced assessment.

"I just kept trying to look at the future and concentrate on what I had to do to get there. Panic is very specific … and I don't think I ever actually panicked. Panic, to me, is undirected action and not being functional. I don't think I suffered from that. For me, the number-one enemy is denial. You have to accept what has happened but not allow it to overwhelm you."

Callahan said though he occasionally became subject to exasperation and even tantrums, he never lost focus on the most important thing.

"You just have to get that frustration out of your system and just deal with what needs to be dealt with."

Callahan said there were several things he wished he had done differently, but overall he felt his pretrip planning was a huge benefit.

According to Callahan, "I made rookie errors. I wasted water and got mad at myself, but looking back. I didn't do that badly. *The only reason I am here is that I took safety at sea seriously* [emphasis mine]. I really tried to prepare myself by having the best equipment I could get at the time."

Callahan said that his tale has helped others in contexts that go beyond a water emergency.

"Surviving in any situation has transferable skills. People have told me that since reading my book they have been able to find comfort and help—and not just in wilderness emergencies or any kind of challenge. Domestic situations and even in dealing with health issues, people have said, 'Your book helped me get through it.'"

It is a difficult proposition to encapsulate just what skills Callahan manifested to survive. There were many instances of his ingenuity (he fixed a catastrophic hole is his raft, for example), but there appear to be several takeaways from his ordeal.

- The daytime use of flares did not have positive results. Multiple ships passed Callahan while he drifted through the Atlantic sea lanes, but he was never observed. The flares were not highly visible during the day, according to Callahan.
- It is difficult, if not impossible, to see a life raft on the water, even if you are actively searching. Callahan said that in his experience in the open ocean, a forty-foot sailboat is difficult to see; a small raft is almost impossible. "It's hard to see anything out there, even if you're looking for it," he recalled.

- As mentioned earlier, water procurement was essential. A desalinator in your survival kit is something that is worth the cost. They are expensive, but if your travels take you offshore, a working desalinator may be the single most important safety item in your raft.
- Having some sense of safety and of the hazards you may face is also essential. Complacency in regard to safety is extremely detrimental and has been proven to be lethal in other sagas. Don't allow yourself to think that it can't happen to you. Regardless of experience and time on the water, "Mother Nature bats last."
- Callahan did have an electronic locator beacon, but the technology was still in its infancy at that time, and satellites did not monitor them. Times have changed, and any electronic locator beacon will be of invaluable service in an emergency.

Callahan is a naval architect by training and holds several patents relating to the marine industry. He still designs and builds boats. He is also a consultant for major motion pictures, including *The Life of Pi* and the Ron Howard film based on the tragedy of the whale ship Essex, *In the Heart of the Sea*. Callahan is also a consultant for the marine safety industry and is available for lectures and speaking engagements. You can find more information at his website, stevencallahan.net.

This article was researched sourcing Callahan's book, *Adrift: 76 Days Lost at Sea*, and from an interview conducted with the author in April 2014.

Twenty-Four Hours in a Life Raft

I once spent twenty-four hours in a life raft, but unlike Callahan's experience, mine was voluntary. My employer at the time had close contacts with survival-equipment companies, and in 2013 I spent twenty-four hours with six others in an experimental raft to test its design and to conduct research into how survivors actually react to sea strandings.

What the adventure reality shows never reveal to you on TV is that despite the illusion of a lone man trapped in the wilderness, fending for himself, there are actually satellite phones, lawyers, camera people, production assistants, and an army of protection for the hosts and participants. Think about it: is the legal team for the Discovery Channel going to place their star in danger? They could never get the insurance to go into production if they did.

Ultimately, that lack of support, that unknown, is what kills people in endurance emergencies. Victims often die from the psychological pressure of the unknown. Some, like Callahan, Aldridge, and Captain Shoemaker, overcome this crushing mental weight, but many do not. We all tried to keep this in mind during this test, but despite the fact we were not in any real danger, we were able to glean some very valuable insights, both practical and psychological.

There are numerous factors to overcome in a real-world situation, and our testing didn't account for injuries or extreme weather that can occur in a real-life disaster. But what we learned includes some practical ideas that may help those stranded at sea to achieve valuable hours of survival time and techniques that can sustain comfort and morale.

The first major issue to arise was simple boredom, which can take effect rather quickly and shouldn't be taken lightly. Whether staring onto an open ocean or a cold gray fog bank, surviving gets tiresome and monotonous quite quickly. Stashing a deck of playing cards in your emergency kit is an excellent idea. Keeping a log book or just pen and paper to jot down thoughts or to maintain a log is also an excellent boredom mitigation device. (If you have the money, most of the major raft companies will customize the raft to include whatever you want to go inside. A bottle of single-malt whiskey, twenty thousand dollars in cash, and a box of condoms are just some of the items I have been told have gone into rafts.)

Many life rafts have only a single opening for the entry, which can cause several problems. One is the lack of air flow, but equally limiting is the lack of additional access points for bodily functions. If a survivor in the back of the raft has to vomit, he would be forced to crawl over the other survivors until he/she reached the front of the raft. This also can be a factor for bathroom breaks. Even with full access around the raft, every time a member had to urinate it caused motion, disturbance, and jostling. With only a single port, this activity could affect morale and increase the likelihood of conflict, especially if survivors are injured. And with only one opening, those stuck in the back of the raft will be hot and far more likely to suffer the effects of seasickness than those with the ability to catch a breeze at the opening. It's important when shopping for life rafts to find one with more than one opening. Most marine rafts will have a zippered portal directly opposite the main boarding area.

During our particular test, there were seven of us in a life raft designed for fourteen people, but we still felt quite crowded and could not all be in the same position (with legs facing the center of the raft) at one time. Most commercially available rafts are built with a 50 percent overfill capacity, which means that as many as twenty-one people should have been able to fit in this model of raft. Even at the limit of fourteen, it would have been extremely difficult to do anything more than scrunch into a fetal position. With seven of us aboard at half capacity, it was still difficult to get comfortable.

Get Comfortable

Comfort raises morale.

We found sponges were handy for several reasons. Most rafts are now equipped with several sponges. It is important to designate a sponge for bailing and a sponge for potable water collection. The ability to soak up every last drop of water inside the raft is not only a comfort issue but is also necessary to prevent hypothermia. A raft with a wet bottom can pull heat away from a survivor at a rapid rate, twenty-five times faster than air. A survivor who makes it into a raft wearing just shorts or just underwear will battle hypothermia in a wet raft, even in warm tropical waters.

During this test in early July off Fishers Island, New York, the air temperature was eighty-three degrees Fahrenheit and the water almost sixty-four degrees. However, mild hypothermia quickly became an issue because as soon as the sun went down, the raft became a very cold and wet place. And we were equipped with top-of-the-line full-immersion suits! It would seem that with an insulated immersion suit in the middle of summer, even with a sea temp of sixty-four degrees, participants would have been protected, but we were still at the mercy of the elements. Though the suits offered protection, dew, sweat, rain, and condensation were enough to bring several participants to the first stage of hypothermia. One of my coworkers and I were shivering quite intensely in the hours just before dawn.

This can be a difficult problem to rectify, as full-immersion suits may be impractical for some crews and are often not donned during a real emergency. However, warmth, even in tropical waters, is essential. Some barrier between you and the surface water is also essential. Many life raft kits come with a Mylar or plastic blanket, and it is recommended that you supplement your kit with at least one for every crew member and more if suitable space can be found.

Without some sort of insulating material, you will quickly become miserable and in danger of hypothermia. Some styles of raft have an inflatable floor that helps keep survivors out of direct contact with the surface water. But no design will keep survivors completely off the surface. More survivors also means more weight and increased contact with the water through the rubber floor. Even with the protection of the floor and an immersion suit, the water quickly pulled heat from us.

Water procurement is the biggest challenge of long-term sea survival. The water collection sponge can be a vital component to staying hydrated. If the raft doesn't have a desalinator or if the device malfunctions, sponges can collect a surprising amount of potable water from condensation and dew that forms on the raft. Make sure your raft is equipped with sponges and, ideally, a desalinator.

Desalinators or other water purifiers should not be sacrificed to save weight. It's a good idea to familiarize yourself with the water-collection devices that are packed in your raft. The system that we tested worked fine until water had to be doled out. The mouth of the bag was too big to allow for a controlled pour, so precious amounts of liquid were spilled. A device with a spigot would have been better. A collapsible cup also would have been useful.

During our test, we poured water into a small plastic bag that had held emergency kit components, and, again, precious drops were lost in the transfer from bag to mouth. It wasn't a big deal during a twenty-four-hour test, but it would be a serious issue in a real emergency, where survivors' lives depend on hydration. It also takes a lot of exertion to make the water. Though we traded off between seven people, it took almost an hour to procure one gallon of water. That's not too bad, but if you are alone, injured, weak, or hypothermic, the amount of energy needed could be difficult to muster.

Raft Stability

Some rudimentary steering and seamanship can be accomplished in rafts. Ballast bags are designed to keep the raft stable in high sea states, but some raft designs allow for the ballast bags to be pulled to the bottom of the raft and tied off. This feature allows the raft to move with the wind more freely without the drag of the bags, which could be useful if the wind is blowing toward shore and the current is headed away from land. Other designs allow these bags to be completely detached and pulled into the raft.

Also, if the bags can be fully removed, they can be used for water collection, sun protection, storage, bailing, a waste bucket, or any creative use survivors conceive. Items with multiple uses are a vital asset on any raft or in any emergency scenario. Remember that ballast bags play an important role in keeping the raft stable in rough conditions so use caution when removing them or tying them off for any reason.

Bug Off!

Biting insects may not sound like a detriment to survival, but during this test, the life raft was a mile offshore, and insects quickly inundated the raft. Flying insects have been documented hundreds of miles from shore, so even open-ocean navigators should be prepared. The best solution would be a combination sunscreen and repellent in one product. The raft was packed with sunscreen wipes that took up little space, but a product that combined an insect repellent would have been helpful.

Shine a Light on It

Adequate lighting is essential. During this test, the raft was almost run over by a small fishing vessel in the wee hours of the morning, despite our safety boat being anchored nearby. The boat never had a chance to see the raft in the heavy fog, and without quick action by a member of the crew, there would have been a collision.

Do not rely on water-activated lights to work. They are notoriously fickle, and when they do work, they often illuminate for only a short time. The design of some water-activated lights allows the batteries to be pulled from the water. If you blow out excess water and dry them, they can be shut off during the day, extending their life and enhancing the chances of rescue.

The items tested included the food, compass, safety knife, and fishing kit. When shopping for a life raft, make sure you know what is included in your life raft's kit, and add additional items before it is packed. It's a good idea to schedule a practice session for your crew to make sure everyone knows how to use it. Get practice on shore before you are actually in an emergency. It's also important for every person on board to know how to work your electronic devices, including GPS units, satellite phones, and beacons.

The best advice I can give is to make sure your life raft and its emergency kit are stocked with everything to make you as comfortable as possible. The addition of a few ounces of emergency equipment may very well save your life and the lives of your crew. All of us in the raft were stunned at how quickly we became miserable and how quickly the morale wavered. And that was with the knowledge that rescue was coming. The more comfortable you are in any emergency, the more likely you are to survive.

Seasickness

"The world can be divided into three classes;
the Living, the Dead, and the Seasick"
—Greek philosopher Anniceris, 300 BCE

If you are working on the water, then it is likely you have established your sea legs. However, enduring your first bout of seasickness while in the midst of an emergency will not increase your chances for survival. Seasickness in a water-based emergency can kill you. Survivors have lived to tell the tale of victims who perished during marine disasters as a result of the mental and physiological complications that result from motion sickness during an emergency.

The nausea associated with motion sickness actually occurs in the brain, according to neurologists. We become nauseated because our brains receive conflicting data—our eyes send signals that we are still, while the equilibrium sensors in our bodies send signals of an environment in motion. This causes a schism between perception and reality and is the reason why humans get nauseated from this phenomenon.

The foremost physical hazard of seasickness is simple dehydration. The violent nausea that normally occurs with most victims can be so intense and overwhelming that people can die from lack of hydration. Dehydration sets off a number of physiological responses, from electrolyte imbalances to blood pressure shifts that can kill a human in a relatively short period of time. This won't occur in minutes, but if prolonged for several hours, especially if injury or prior dehydration is an issue, it can be fatal.

The mental degradations of seasickness, though harder to quantify, are actually more critical in regard to sea survival. There are, unfortunately, numerous case histories of people overcome by seasickness who perished because they gave up the will to survive. The diminished mental capability that seasickness causes can be so psychologically devastating that your ability to assist in your own survival and that of others is severely compromised. If a group of struggling survivors must perform a task or prepare a plan, and you are so incapacitated that you cannot join in the effort, you may be left off the list. If your sickness begins to overwhelm or interfere in the survival of others, you will not survive.

"The will to live turns to a wish to die," according to many who have survived these crises.

In 1988 workers on the Rowan Gorilla One oil rig in the North Atlantic were forced to abandon the rig after sixty-foot waves began to collapse the platform. All twenty-six men made it into a life boat, and all became seasick after just moments inside the confines of the rigid-style escape pod (picture a great big Advil tablet). Interviews with survivors made it abundantly clear that their sickness impaired them mentally and physically, to the point where their lives were in danger. Several recall wishing that the waves would destroy the life boat and consume them all, just so their misery could end.[4]

I've spent my life on the water, and I never had a bout of motion sickness due to the sea until I became a sea-survival instructor. According to medical professionals, as we age the fluid in the middle ear thickens, making some people more prone to various forms of motion sickness. I cannot offer any concrete advice on products that prevent or mitigate seasickness, as most have not worked for me.

I have advanced medical training, but I am not a doctor, and I cannot recommend or dissuade readers from certain products or techniques. I can, however, offer my personal experience and those of students I have instructed. However, you should consult your doctor before taking any product. Over-the-counter motion sickness products can interact with several different medications.

A standard dose of two pills of dimenhydrinate effectively prevents my motion sickness, but it makes me so exhausted and drowsy that I can't effectively function. I become so incapacitated by the recommended dose that I have concerns as to whether I could function in an emergency. This is probably not the psychological state you want to be in when struggling for your survival. Even a half dose, one tablet, still has a strong sedative effect on me. By reducing the dose to just a quarter of the recommended one, half of one tablet, I remain sickness-free and still able to function. Whether this is a placebo effect, I cannot discern, but I do know that I get seasick if I do not take some level of antimotion sickness medicine.

Meclizine seems to work better for some people, in that it causes less drowsiness in the system, but many still feel quite exhausted from the full recommended dose of this product. As with other products, I take a quarter of the recommended dose.

There is also a prescription medication called scopolamine (Scopace), which is usually taken by transdermal patch. Many claim scopolamine is very effective in the treatment of motion sickness. It was taken off the market by the manufacturer in the 1990s to address some of the side effects. It is now available again by prescription in patch and tablet form. Recent studies are suggesting that the pill form is more effective for many users.

I am aware of more than a dozen motion-sickness remedies. No other product that I have found—clamps, bands, ginger, or other medication—has worked for me. A small dose of commercial over-the-counter products is the only thing that has mitigated my symptoms, although there are many people who claim relief from these alternative remedies. I have tested them and found no beneficial effect. I must emphasize that I ordinarily suffer only mild or moderate seasickness, so my personal recommendations may be of little value to others. However, it may be a rough guideline to find the right dosage for you.

The classic advice of fixing your gaze on the horizon does work for me if I feel sickness coming on, but if it is dark or if I'm confined by weather inside a vessel or raft, this technique doesn't afford any relief. Once you have become sick, fixing on the horizon will not be effective.

The products mentioned above have potentially serious interactions with other medications, including common OTC analgesics. Never mix medications of any kind without consulting a doctor.

I recommend administering seasickness medications to survivors as quickly as possible in a life raft. Once survivors have begun to get sick, they obviously will not be able to keep down any medication, which will compound their sickness. Once people have begun to succumb to the effects of motion sickness, the only way to administer medicine is rectally. Not only will this be difficult in a raft, but the effectiveness of the dosage will decrease. The body will not absorb the medication as quickly, and its distribution through the bloodstream will not be as effective.

In the close confines of a canopied life raft, the stench of vomit also will affect everyone inside. If one person vomits, no matter how inured you are to seasickness, you are probably going to get sick yourself. Also, the smell of industrial glues and adhesives can be nauseating, and the adrenaline coursing through your body can compound this feeling as well.

Recap: seasickness can be fatal in the depths of a marine emergency. Preplan for yourself and your crew for this occurrence. Make sure that your emergency life raft kit has seasickness medication and that all crew know where the remedy tablets are located so they can be administered quickly and effectively. In my experience as a survival instructor, one of the shortest durations of time is the length between someone saying, "I have never been seasick" and the sound of vomit hitting the water. Regardless of how iron-cast your stomach is or how long you've been on the water, especially during an emergency, anyone is susceptible to motion sickness.

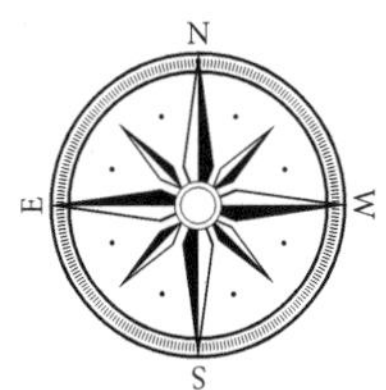

Survival Psychology

Who lives and who dies in an emergency, and why?

Often, pure luck, good or bad, determines a survivor's fate, and that never can be accurately quantified. However, in general, the science does allow for some insights into the answer to this question. (For a complete background on this topic, I would highly recommend Laurence Gonzales's *Deep Survival*, Ben Sherwood's *Survivor's Club*, Frank Golden and Michael Tipton's *Essentials of Sea Survival*, and, of course, Steven Callahan's *76 Days Adrift*. I refer to and cite all of these works throughout this book.)

In the United States there are between 3,300 and 4,000 water-related deaths reported every year; worldwide, there are more than 140,000.[1] Though most of these fatalities do not encompass long-term sea strandings, every year navigators and survivors are rescued after exceedingly long periods adrift on the waves.

So how do people endure epic survivals, especially long periods at sea, or even short-term life-threatening scenarios? And how can their experiences help us survive less epic but nonetheless dire emergencies?

In 1966, Dennis Hale was the sole survivor of a tragic sinking that left him in forty-degree water for forty hours during a gale on Lake Huron—a tale so incredible that some simply didn't believe him. Stephen Callahan survived seventy-six days alone at sea in a life raft; Bill and Simonne Butler survived sixty-six days in a raft; Maurice and Maralyn Bailey lasted 117 days in their life raft before rescue.

After they were cast adrift by a mutinous crew in 1789, the infamous Captain Bligh and eighteen others of the HMS *Bounty* sailed more than 3,600 nautical miles before they made landfall in Timor (in an overloaded open launch with the gunwales only inches above the water). In 1916 explorer Ernest Shackleton navigated more than eight hundred miles in a twenty-foot open boat across the Weddell Sea. He and some of his crew survived hurricane-force winds that sunk other, much larger vessels, and then Shackleton undertook a monumental mountain trek over South Georgia Island to reach rescue. Then he promptly turned around and did the whole return journey to help save the remainder of his crew left stranded on the ice.[2]

The tales and strategies of these survivors are as varied as their backgrounds. Some survived on sheer determination; some used MacGyver-like skills and knowledge; others were just plain lucky.

One of the most incredible tales of survival is of Isabel Godin des Odonais, a Peruvian noblewoman who was the sole survivor of an ill-fated attempt to navigate three thousand miles of the Amazon River in 1769. According to author Robert Whitaker, in his well-researched book, *The Mapmaker's Wife*, every other member of the forty-two-person expedition, including Isabel's brothers, succumbed to the hazards of the jungle. Somehow, this woman of refined tastes and of little outdoor experience was able to crawl out of the jungle after more than a month on her own. Her tale is truly inspirational and almost defies belief.[3] (After their marriage, her husband left to set up their new home in France in 1749, and his tale is equally fraught with danger, imprisonment, intrigue, and just plain bad luck. It took more than twenty years for the two lovers to finally set eyes on each other again, having had almost no word of the other's fate. They eventually reunited in Paris, where both died the same year.)

Dennis Hale's sole survivor saga is another unbelievable tale of overcoming the odds. According to Hale, for more than twenty years he refused to speak of the disaster on Lake Huron because of the negative response he sometimes encountered. According to official records, Hale was a watchman on the six-hundred-foot bulk freighter SS *Daniel J. Morrell.* It ran headlong into a November gale on Lake Huron and broke in half during the storm. In what can only be called bizarre bad luck, the remaining crewmen were huddled in the forward section of the ship, seeking refuge, when shouts arose that another vessel had been spotted. It was actually the aft section of the *Morrell*, still under power and barreling toward the survivors. It smashed into the bow section, forcing the men into the frigid lake waters.

Hale made it onto some wreckage with three others, wearing only his boxer shorts and a peacoat. While the others eventually perished, he survived close to forty hours in thirty-nine-degree water in a howling gale. Disbelief prevailed because it was thought impossible for a human to survive that long in such extreme conditions. (For a full accounting of Hale's tale, read *Shipwrecked: Reflections of a Sole Survivor.*)[4]

How is it that a pampered woman in 1769 survives a trek that routinely kills hardened explorers to this day, and Dennis Hale survives his ordeal while a US Navy SEAL dies of hypothermia during an overnight training exercise?

Training, mental toughness, and experience all seem to play a part in survival. Stress inoculation—a term coined by several branches of the US military—reveals that repeated high-fidelity training improves the odds of survival. However, with case histories of Hale and Odonais, clearly there are other factors that play.

So what are they, and can they be quantified and taught?

Like many insightful questions, the answer is yes and no, but it is possible to glean information from these tales.

How people react in an emergency tends to break down into the following groups, according to Dr. John Leach, one of the pioneers of survival psychology.

- Ten to 15 percent will be leaders. They will act calmly and rationally and be able to provide valuable leadership and control.
- Roughly 70 percent of us will be sheep. We won't be able to take control during an emergency and lead, but we will be able to follow commands and take part in the survival of ourselves and others.
- Another 10–15 percent will panic. They will act inappropriately and irrationally and provide no assistance to themselves or others, and in some cases they will interfere with the survival of others.[5]

In many cases, survivors in the panic group simply freeze. This is part of negative panic or *incredulity response*. Many people have heard of fight-or-flight, but "freeze" is the most common reaction to fear. Numerous case histories cite people in this state being slapped, kicked, and punched as fire consumes them or as they go down with the ship, resisting all efforts to save them or to recognize the danger.[6]

We don't necessarily remain fixed in one group or the other. As the emergency intensifies or abates, survivors can shift from one group to another during a crisis. Just because we reacted well to one emergency doesn't mean we are permanently part of the leader group. (I once kept my head after finding myself a quarter-mile offshore in twenty-foot waves and thirty-four-degree water in Lake Michigan. A few years later I completely lost my marbles when I accidently stuck a chainsaw into my leg.)

So what can we learn?

If you have access to high-intensity training, that is never a bad thing. Data demonstrates that high-stress training will improve your odds of survival. It is not a guarantee, but numerous training scenarios across the full spectrum of the US military indicate that test subjects can become inured to the stress of emergencies, which can significantly increase their chances of survival.

Dr. Charles Morgan III of Yale University has conducted testing in cooperation with several US military branches that has uncovered evidence that high-stress training will improve the odds of survival. Levels of stress hormones associated with the fear response have been shown to be counteracted by the release of neuropeptides in test subjects who have undergone intense high-fidelity training. In some respects these peptides act as a natural tranquilizer and allow for better cognitive function; they also appear to function as a stress buffer.[7] Data also indicate that these subjects return to a "normal" level of peptides post-training more quickly than others. In fact, through Morgan's analysis, he claims he can now predict, with a high degree of accuracy, those who will perform better during this training and those who will not.

So what does that mean for the average Joe who doesn't have access to a military resistance training laboratory or is too busy paying the bills to take off on an adventure fantasy camp halfway around the globe?

According to several of these studies, it is their conclusion that training on any level, regardless of its intensity, is beneficial. A simple dockside brief before the start of the season or a trip to sea can be a valuable asset. Having a plan, thinking through possible emergency scenarios, and understanding how to use safety and survival equipment have all been proven to be beneficial in emergencies. Though high-fidelity and intense training will increase survival rates, that doesn't mean less stressful training is worthless.

In short, any training is better than none. And preparation can be far more beneficial than any level of training. Preventing the emergency from occurring in the first place, so that you won't need to fight a rip current or eat fish eyeballs in a life raft, is the only true antidote to disaster. However, if you find yourself in an emergency despite proper preparation, certain actions can save you.

In survival training we refer to the classic dilemma: how do you eat an elephant?

The answer: one bite at a time.

You can't survive all at once; you have to tackle it one step at a time. Knowing and understanding basic hypothermia mitigation and first aid can save lives. Familiarity with all items and components of your survival kit and safety equipment also will save lives.

Perhaps most important, don't sink into the depths of despair or allow others to do so. Don't become so excited with positivity that you exhaust your mental reserves. (Optimists, oddly, are many times the first to perish in emergencies. See the discussion of the Stockdale Paradox in chapter 6 for further information on this counterintuitive response.)

According to one expert, combining a blunt appreciation of the predicament with a steadfast belief of survival, or "realistic optimism," is the most critical psychological factor in survival.

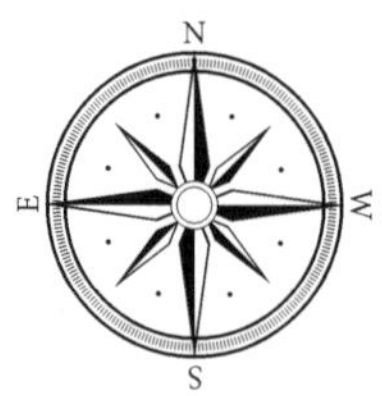

Conclusion

We've covered a lot in this book, and my intention was to prevent it from being overwhelming. I tried to impart every bit of knowledge and experience I have accumulated over the course of my career and my time in the water. As such, there are sections that are not applicable to every person in or on the water. Most of us will never put on an immersion suit or face a Callahan-like sea stranding. I believe, however, even the casual beachgoer can implement the valuable information in this guide. Get in the water and have fun, but stay safe! Just a moment of reflection or introspection can save a life.

Remember:

- Prevent the emergency.
- Recognize the dangers of water, including pools.
- Understand cold-water immersion and hypothermia.
- Use the HELP and carpet formations.
- Stay away from swift water.
- Don't swim for it.
- Understand rip currents.
- Know your equipment.

Notes

Preface

1 USCG Fatality Stats 2009, accessed June 28, 2017, http://uscgboating.org/statistics/accident_statistics.php/.
2 Centers for Disease Control, *Death Statistics and Fatality Statistics*, accessed June 28, 2017, https://www.cdc.gov/homeandrecreationalsafety/water-safety/waterinjuries-factsheet.html/.
3 Frank Pia, *On Drowning* (New York: Water Safety Films, Inc.), http://www.pia-enterprises.com.html/.
4 USA Today, February 12, 2012, accessed June 28,, 2017, .http://content.usatoday.com/communities/ondeadline/post/2011/06/drowning-victim-not-found-in-mass-pool-for-2-days/1#.WVQmpjGWyMI/.

Chapter 1

1 B. Latane and J. Darley, "Bystander 'Apathy,'" American Scientist 57 (1969): 244–268.
2 Ibid., 244–268.

Chapter 2

1 Centers for Disease Control, Death Statistics and Fatality Statistics, accessed June 28,, 2017,https://www.cdc.gov/homeandrecreationalsafety/water-safety/waterinjuries-factsheet.html/.

2 Ibid.

3 G. J. Wintemute, "Childhood Drowning and Near-Drowning in the United States," *American Journal of Diseases of Children* 144, no. 6 (1990): 663–669, http://www.jamanetwork.com/journals/jamapediatrics/fullarticle/515182.html/.

4 Jeremy S. H. Jackson and Roger Blackman, "A Driving-Simulator Test of Wilde's Risk Homeostasis Theory" (PDF), *Journal of Applied Psychology* (1994).

5 Centers for Disease Control, *Death Statistics and Fatality Statistics*, accessed June 28, 2017. https://www.cdc.gov/homeandrecreationalsafety/water-safety/waterinjuries-factsheet.html/.

Chapter 3

1 Gordon Giesbrecht and James A. Wilkerson, Hypothermia, Frostbite and Other Cold Emergencies (Seattle: Mountaineers Press, 2006), 58.

2 Ibid., 23–30.

3 Ibid., 8–9.

4 Ibid., 23–30.

5 Ibid., 57–65.

6 Ibid.

7 Al Siebert, *The Survivor Personality* (New York: Tarcher-Perigee, 2010), 10–15.

8 Giesbrecht and Wilkerson, *Hypothermia, Frostbite and Other Cold Emergencies*, 64–66.

9 Ibid., 18.

10 Ibid., 59.

11 Ian Sample, "Scientists Debunk Myth That You Lose Most Heat through Your Head," *Guardian*, December 17, 2008.

12 Giesbrecht and Wilkerson, *Hypothermia, Frostbite and Other Cold Emergencies*, 68.

13 Ibid., 39–47.

14 Ibid., 63–65.

15 Ibid., 24, 27.

16 Ibid., 38–56.

17 17. Ibid.

18 Ibid.

19 B. Wedin, L. Vanggaard, and J. Hirvonen, "'Paradoxical Undressing' in Fatal Hypothermia," *Journal of Forensic Science* (July 1, 1979), accessed June 28,, 2017, http://onlinelibrary.wiley.com/journal.html/.

20 Giesbrecht and Wilkerson, *Hypothermia, Frostbite and Other Cold Emergencies*, 62.

21 National Oceanic and Atmospheric Administrations: Centers for Environmental Information, accessed March 1, 2017, http://www.noaa.gov/data.html/.

Chapter 4

1 United States Coast Guard, "Boater Survey Report" (2012), accessed June 28, 2017. http://uscgboating.org/library/recreational-boating-servey/2012survey%20report.pdf/.

2 New York Times., "Plane Is Hijacked; Crashes in Ocean off East Africa," Accessed June 28, 2017. http://www.nytimes.com/1996/11/24/world/plane-is-hijacked-crashes-in-ocean-off-east-africa.html/.

3 USCG, *Think Safe Life Vest Recommendations* (2009), accessed June 28, 2017, .http://www.uscg.mil/hq/cg5/cg5214/pfdselection.asp/.

4 DAN (Divers Alert Network), "Annual Diving Report" (PDF) (2008, 2009), accessed December 20, 2016, http://www.diversalertnetwork.org/research.html/.

Chapter 5

1 Giesbrecht and Wilkerson, Hypothermia, Frostbite and Other Cold Emergencies, 64–66.

2 CDC, "Unintentional Drowning: Get the Facts," accessed January 15, 2017, https://www.cdc.gov/homeandrecreationalsafety/water-safety/waterinjuries-factsheet.html/..

3 Stuart Holmes Coleman, introduction to *Eddie Would Go: The Story of Eddie Aikau. Hawaiian Hero and Pioneer of Big Wave Surfing* (New York: St. Martin's Press, 2004).

4 National Weather Service Rip Current Awareness Page, accessed January 15, 2017, http://www.ripcurrents.noaa.gov.html/.

5 Ibid.

6 AAP with Amy Middleton, "Rips More Dangerous than Bushfires or Sharks," *Australian Geographic* (November 26, 2013).

Chapter 6

1 Giesbrecht and Wilkerson, Hypothermia, Frostbite and Other Cold Emergencies, 18.
2 James C. Collins, *Good to Great: Why Some Companies Make the Leap ... and Others Don't* (New York: Harper Business, 2001), 101–103.
3 Al Siebert, introduction to *The Survivor Personality* (New York: Tarcher-Perigee, 2010).
4 J. P. Landolt, I. M. Light, M. G. Greenen, and C. Monaco, "Seasickness in Totally-Enclosed Motor-Propelled Survival Craft: Five Offshore Oil Rig Disasters," *Aviation, Space, and Environmental Medicine* 63, no. 2 (February 1992): 138–144.

Chapter 7

1 Centers for Disease Control, Death Statistics and Fatality Data, accessed June 28, 2017, https://www.cdc.gov/homeandrecreationalsafety/water-safety/waterinjuries-factsheet.html/.
2 Dennis Perkins, *Leading at the Edge: Leadership Lessons from the Extraordinary Saga of Shackleton's Antarctica Expedition* (New York: AMACOM, 2000), 101–105.
3 Robert Whitaker, introduction to *The Mapmaker's Wife* (Basic Books, 2016).
4 Dennis Hale, introduction to *Shipwrecked: Reflections of a Sole Survivor* (Dennis Hale, 2010).
5 John Leach, *Survival Psychology* (New York: New York University Press, 1994).
6 Ibid.
7 Charles A. Morgan III, Sheila Wang, John Mason, Steven M. Southwick, Patrick Fox, Gary Hazlett, Dennis S. Charney, and Gary Greenfield, "Hormone Profiles in Humans Experiencing Military Survival Training," in *Stress and the Brain: The Science of Mental Health*, ed. Steven Hyman (2001).

Selected Bibliography

AAP with Amy Middleton. "Rips More Dangerous than Bushfires or Sharks." *Australian Geographic*, November 27, 2013.

Callahan, Steven. *Adrift: 76 Days Adrift*. New York: Mariner Books, 2002.

Centers for Disease Control. www.cdc.gov/faststats/.

Coleman, Stuart Holmes. *Eddie Would Go: The Story of Eddie Aikau. Hawaiian Hero and Pioneer of Big Wave Surfing*. New York: St. Martin's Press, 2004.

Collins, James C. *Good to Great: Why Some Companies Make the Leap ... and Others Don't*. New York: Harper Business, 2001.

Giesbrecht, Gordon, and James A. Wilkerson. *Hypothermia, Frostbite and Other Cold Emergencies*. Seattle: Mountaineers Press, 1986–2006.

Golden, Frank, and Michael Tipton. *The Essentials of Sea Survival*. Human Kinetics, 2002.

Gonzales, Laurence. *Deep Survival*. New York: W. W. Norton and Company, 2005.

Hale, Dennis. *Shipwrecked: Reflections of a Sole Survivor.* Dennis Hale, 2010.

Hillenbrand, Laura. *Unbroken: A World War Two Story of Survival, Resilience, and Redemption.* New York, 2014.

Jackson, Jeremy S. H., and Roger Blackman. "A Driving-Simulator Test of Wilde's Risk Homeostasis Theory" (PDF). *Journal of Applied Psychology* (1994).

Kantar, Andrew. *Deadly Voyage.* East Lansing: University of Michigan Press, 2010.

Koepcke, Juliane. "How I Survived a Plane Crash." BBC News. March 24, 2012. Retrieved January 24, 2017.

Landolt, J. P., I. M. Light, M. G. Greenen, and C. Monaco. "Seasickness in Totally-Enclosed Motor-Propelled Survival Craft: Five Offshore Oil Rig Disasters." *Aviation, Space, and Environmental Medicine* 63, no. 2 (February 1992): 138–144.

Latane, B., and J. Darley. "Bystander 'Apathy,'" *American Scientist* 57 (1969): 244–268.

Leach, John. *Survival Psychology.* New York: New York University Press, 1994.

Morgan, Charles A. III, Sheila Wang, John Mason, Steven M. Southwick, Patrick Fox, Gary Hazlett, Dennis S. Charney, and Gary Greenfield. "Hormone Profiles in Humans Experiencing Military Survival Training." In *Stress and the Brain: The Science of Mental Health,* edited by Steven Hyman., 2001.

Nelson, Jack. *Flashes in the Night.* Loyola University Press, Maryland: Apprentice House, 2010.

National Weather Service Rip Current Awareness Page. www.ripcurrents.noaa.gov/.

National Oceanic and Atmospheric Administrations: Centers for Environmental Information. www.noaa.gov/.

Perkins, Dennis. *Leading at the Edge: Leadership Lessons from the Extraordinary Saga of Shackleton's Antarctica Expedition.* New York: AMACOM, 2000.

Perrow, Charles. *Normal Accidents.* New Jersey: Princeton University Press, 1999.

Pia, Frank. *On Drowning.* New York: Water Safety Films, Inc.

Rochester, Stuart I, and Frederick Kiley. *Honor Bound: American Prisoners of War in Southeast Asia, 1961–1973.* Naval Institute Press, 1999.

Sabella, John. *After the Galaxy: The Legacy Lives On.* With David Shoemaker. John Sabella and Associates Publishing, 2013.

Sagan, Scott D. *The Limits of Safety.* New Jersey: Princeton University Press, 1993.

Sherwood, Ben. *The Survivors Club.* New York: Grand Central Publishing, 2009.

Siebert, Al. *The Survivor Personality.* New York: Tarcher-Perigee, 2010.

Whitaker, Robert. *The Mapmaker's Wife.* Basic Books, 2016.

Wedin, B., L. Vanggaard, and J. Hirvonen. "'Paradoxical Undressing' in Fatal Hypothermia." *Journal of Forensic Science* (July 1979).

Wintemute, G. J. "Childhood Drowning and Near-Drowning in the United States." *American Journal of Diseases of Children* 144, no. 6 (1990): 663–669.

The Committee on Injury and Poison Prevention. *Physician's Resource Guide for Water Safety Education*. American Academy of Pediatrics, June 1994.

USCG Fatality Stats, 2009. (Also, archives and published public material.) www.uscg.gov/.

USCG. *Think Safe Life Vest Recommendations*. 2009.

Printed in the United States
By Bookmasters